HAL MOORE
ON ★★★ LEADERSHIP

WINNING WHEN OUTGUNNED AND OUTMANNED

LT GEN HAROLD G. MOORE (USA, RET)
MIKE GUARDIA

Published by Magnum Books
Maple Grove, MN

ISBN: 978-15483051-0-9

For Marie, Melanie,
and the serving and retired members of the US Armed Forces

Also by Mike Guardia:

American Guerilla
Shadow Commander
Hal Moore: A Soldier Once...and Always
The Fires of Babylon

Also by Lt. Gen. Harold G. Moore

We Were Soldiers Once...and Young
We Are Soldiers Still

TABLE OF CONTENTS

Prologue   vii

Introduction   ix

Chapter 1 – The Four Basic Principles of Leadership   1

Chapter 2 – Call of Duty   9

Chapter 3 – Learning the Ropes   29

Chapter 4 – Trial by Fire   49

Chapter 5 – Vietnam   97

Chapter 6 – The Guiding Hand   115

Epilogue – Stacking Up: Moore's Officer Evaluation Reports   136

Appendix A: Lieutenant Leadership in Combat   143

Appendix B: "We Shall Prevail"   147

Appendix C: "Without Equal"   151

PROLOGUE

All of one's life is a <u>learning experience</u>

I've learned a lot of lessons along the way. I'm still learning.

For many years, I've been giving talks on Leadership with the theme "Values in Action." These are values, principles, lessons I've learned, mistakes, successes, and my thoughts on leadership from watching, studying and reading about leaders in action—good leaders, mediocre leaders, bad leaders. I've talked to military, athletic teams, business and student audiences and what I say has been well received.

This book is not an autobiography. It's not a "how to" book on military leadership, the chapters include selected periods in my life. Covered will be leaders, leadership, and experiences which made life-long impressions on me; and lessons learned— most of which have application in all fields of endeavor.

HAROLD G. MOORE
Lt. General, USA-Ret.
January 2002

With those words scrawled in longhand on a yellow legal pad, our father began writing the history of his life as a leader. 13,226 words later, he had created seven chapters of an amazingly detailed, candid draft tracing his evolution as a leader across different phases of his life. Our mother, the only person who could read his handwriting with precision, painstakingly typed each word into Microsoft Word; saved on the old Dell computer our brother, Steve Moore gave them in 1997.

Sadly, that is where the documents lay for years as life got in the way. The heart-shattering early death of our mother at age 75 in 2004 and the need to finish the sequel to *We Were Soldiers Once... And Young* moved this project to the back burner.

Unlike old soldiers who fade away, computers just die. Steve had the task of recovering the files and, in doing so, discovered the bones of this book. Recognizing it as a treasure, the family's challenge was to find an accomplished writer who could take the project across the finish line. Enter Mike Guardia, an internationally recognized author and military historian who has been nominated twice for the Army Historical Foundation's Distinguished Book Award as well as being a finalist for the International Book Award in the Military category.

Mike's introduction to Dad was the movie, *We Were Soldiers*, which he saw on opening night in 2002. *We Were Soldiers* was remarkable to him because it was the first film he had seen to portray a Vietnam veteran in a positive light. For years, his generation had grown up on *Platoon, Full Metal Jacket, The Deer Hunter, Apocalypse Now*, and *Casualties of War*—all of which portrayed the Vietnam veteran as malicious, mentally unstable, or a misfit in modern society. *We Were Soldiers*, however, had no political agenda. It was an honest and intimate portrayal of the men who fought valiantly in Southeast Asia.

In the years following the film's release, he read Dad's books—*We Were Soldiers Once...and Young, We Are Soldiers Still*—and was surprised to learn that no one had written Dad's biography. After extensive vetting by the family, Mike started to work on that project with full access to Dad and unrestricted use of his personal archives including a wealth of personal papers, speeches, photographs, government documents, and war trophies. The resulting work, *Hal Moore: A Soldier Once...and Always*, was released in late 2013 and received critical acclaim.

There was no better person to finish the job and the family is grateful to him for taking on the challenge.

-The Moore Family

INTRODUCTION

The men of 1st Battalion, 7th Cavalry were standing strong in the face of enemy fire. They had been on Landing Zone X-Ray for only a few hours and already their worst scenario was coming to pass: the Americans were outnumbered, understrength, and one of their platoons had been cut off and its leadership killed. To make matters worse, the friendly reinforcements were tied to the helicopters' timeline—a 20-minute round trip. Meanwhile, their commander, Lieutenant Colonel Harold G. "Hal" Moore kept his wits about him as he set up his "command post" at a nearby termite mound. Trying his best to ignore the gunshots, screams, and the bullets whipping past his head, he calmly called for artillery suppression on the menacing North Vietnamese. This would be the first major battle between the United States Army and the People's Army of North Vietnam—and would go down in history as one of the bloodiest engagements of the Vietnam War. But this battle was not the first leadership challenge that Hal Moore had faced…nor would it be his last.

Hal Moore led his life by a set of principles—a code developed through years of experience, trial-and-error, and the study of leaders of every stripe. In a career spanning more than thirty years, Moore's life touched upon many historical events: the Occupation of Japan, the Korean War, Vietnam, and the re-fashioning of the US Army into an all-volunteer force. At each juncture, he learned critical lessons and had opportunities to affect change through measured responses. *Hal Moore on Leadership* offers a comprehensive guide to the principles that helped shape Moore's success both on and off the battlefield. They are strategies for the outnumbered, outgunned, and seemingly hopeless. They apply to any leader in any organization. These lessons and principles are nothing theoretical or scientific. They are simply rules of thumb learned and practiced by a man who spent his entire adult life leading others and perfecting his art of leadership.

We live in a time when our nation is crying out for leadership. Throughout the past decade, we've heard that if America had "better leadership" during our wars in Iraq and Afghanistan, both conflicts could have been resolved quickly—or avoided entirely. We often hear that poor "business leadership" caused the economic downturn of the 2000s and 2010s. Yet, for as often as we clamor for a leader, the real definition of "leadership" remains elusive. For instance, Webster's Collegiate Dictionary—the gold standard for the English lexicon—defines leadership simply as "a position of a leader of a group" or "the capacity to lead."

Although leadership may be difficult to define, Hal Moore certainly knew what leadership was not. For instance, he did not subscribe to the notion that leaders are "managers." During the 1950s (when Moore was rising through the Army's mid-level ranks), there was a popular adage that said: "a manager is a leader." Managers are simply those who can run systems and yield results. Most of us have known people who were great managers but were bad leaders because they forgot the fundamental component of their organization—*people*. Hal Moore knew that leaders lead people—people with hopes, dreams, and ambitions. Without people, all the high-tech gadgetry and technical know-how would be rendered useless.

When Moore commanded an airmobile battalion in Vietnam, the helicopters that delivered them into battle wouldn't move an inch without the right pilots to fly them. The M–16 Assault Rifle would never fire a shot without a trained marksman behind it. Moore understood that his people were his greatest asset. As with any asset, the leader must spend a lot of time and energy to ensure that it functions. Nurturing these assets and cultivating the right relationships is what led to success in every unit that Hal Moore commanded.

Moore also understood the challenge of leadership: inspiring people to work hard and to execute tasks *willingly*. To meet that challenge, a leader must demonstrate three things: (1) He must be competent, (2) he must exercise good judgment, and (3) he must have character. By itself, competence is meaningless without character and good judgment. If one were to look at the greatest leadership failures of the past 100 years, it would be clear they were not failures of *competence*; they were failures of *character* and *judgment*. For example, in 2001, the chief executives at Enron were exposed for their massive accounting fraud, which led to the company's demise. Kenneth Lay and his cohorts were among the most competent business leaders in the world, yet their poor judgment and duplicity (a lack of character) destroyed the company; disrupting the lives of their employees and shareholders.

In the realm of leadership, character and judgment are paramount. Indeed, the ethics and moral climate of any organization are established at the higher echelons. Creating a robust ethical climate is exactly what Moore strove to do in the organizations he led. More than once, he took over a unit suffering from toxic leadership. Each time, Moore relished the opportunity to take command of a depressed organization. He often said: "If given a chance to take a bad unit or a good unit, I will take the bad unit every time. They have nowhere to go but up." Yet for Hal Moore, being a leader did not always mean being loved. He often had to make unpopular decisions. And though he may not always have been loved, he was always respected by those he led because (a) he never held his men to a standard he could not meet himself and (b) he took responsibility for his own actions and the actions of the organization.

Throughout this book, Moore's highlighted leadership lessons appear either in **bold** text or as items within a bulleted list. I am once again indebted to the Moore family and to Joe Galloway for their unyielding support and hospitality. They were instrumental in helping me gather the information for *Hal Moore: A Soldier Once…and Always* and were equally supportive of the work to create *Hal Moore on Leadership*.

In a career that spanned more than thirty years, Harold G. Moore proved himself to be a remarkable leader. This is the story of his leadership.

Hal Moore routinely interacted with business and sports organizations to inspire action and teach. One of the teams Moore supported was the St. Louis Cardinals and their manager, Tony La Russa. At spring training in 2006, he worked with the team to amplify the winning spirit that La Russa had already injected into the team culture. At the end of Moore's time with the team, he confidently told them they would win the World Series. La Russa responded that Moore would get a ring along with the rest of the team when they won. The Cardinals beat the Detroit Tigers and the inset on the picture shows La Russa presenting Moore his World Series ring. *Photo given to the Moore family by the City of Auburn*

THE FOUR BASIC PRINCIPLES
OF LEADERSHIP

I am in the winter of my life now, and I have spent much of it leading people, reading people, leading myself, being led, and reading about leaders. Years ago, during my combat service in the Korean War, I developed four basic principles of leadership. While learned in war, they apply in business, in government, in athletic competitions, in the home, in the family—anywhere.

Principle #1: Three strikes and you're not out.

In the game of baseball, three strikes and you're out. Not so in the game of life. Three strikes and you're *not* out. There are two things a leader can do: he can either contaminate his environment (and his people) with his attitude and actions, or he can inspire confidence. A leader must be visible to the people he leads. He must be self-confident and always maintain a positive attitude. If a leader thinks he might lose in whatever crisis or situation; *then he has already lost.* He must exhibit a determination to prevail no matter what the odds or how difficult the situation. He must have and display the *will to prevail* by his actions, his words, his tone of voice, his appearance, his demeanor, his countenance, and the look in his eyes. He must never give off any hint or evidence that he is uncertain about a positive outcome.

It struck me early in my reading in school and in later life that a common theme running through books and stories about great leaders was their positive outlook; their positive mental attitude. They were aware of the pitfalls and the negatives, but they refused to fret and worry

m. Rather, they dwelt on how to get the job done and done
e the traps and snares along the way. Good leaders make it
dentify and find those traps, snares, ambushes and avoid or
..cm. A leader's behavior, poise, appearance, vision, demeanor,
presence," aura, his manner of speaking and listening—all reflect the
person within; his principles and values. A leader sets the tone and
attitude for his people. Therefore, it's important to exude honest and
fully qualified self-confidence, and unwavering commitment to be the
best; to accept no less. Some people are born with that encoded, self-
assured gene and are naturally confident in their abilities to shape the
future, make the right decisions and succeed. But it can be developed in
others.

Here are two examples from the world of sports. Joe Montana was one
of the greatest quarterbacks in the history of football. In tough situations
with time running out on the clock, he had a unique ability to inspire
the team and go on to win. In the 1989 Super Bowl, Montana's team,
the San Francisco 49ers were three points behind with 3:20 left in the
fourth quarter. He led the 49ers a full 92 yards, throwing for the winning
touchdown pass with only 34 seconds left in the game. It was one of
Montana's 31 fourth-quarter "come from behind" victories. Joe Namath
was another great quarterback in American football. Three days before
his team, the upstart New York Jets, were scheduled to play the Baltimore
Colts in the 1969 Super Bowl, Namath announced to the world that the
21-point underdog Jets would win, saying: "I guarantee it!"

Final score: Jets 16, Colts 7.

Namath exuded self-confidence and a positive attitude.

Principle #2: There's always one more thing you can do to influence any situation in your favor. And after that, there's one more thing.

And after that, there's one more thing. And after that, one more thing.
The more 'One More Things' you do, the better your chances are for
achieving success in any situation. A leader must create time to detach
himself mentally and ask: *"What am I doing that I should not be doing? And
what am I not doing that I should be doing to influence the situation in my
favor?"* A leader (whether a junior leader or senior executive) is paid to
do three things:

1. **Get the job done and get it done well.**

2. Plan ahead—be proactive, not reactive.

3. Exercise good, sound judgment in doing all of the above.

To get the job done, the leader must have a clearly-defined mission along with specific goals and objectives. He must have a clear understanding of a variety of factors which could affect mission accomplishment. He must have a workable plan to accomplish his mission and a system for measuring progress. Most importantly, his people—especially his subordinate leaders—must understand the plan, their individual objectives, and how the pieces fit together to carry out their parts.

The leader must know his primary challenges and how those challenges may impact his command or his unit. He must understand the playing field; and he must know his own capabilities. To produce a realistic plan of action, he must first make an honest assessment of the situation. What are the assets, constraints, strong points, weak areas, etc? How can the "minuses" be turned into "pluses?" What are the essential things that must be done? What are the frills—the things that are nice to have but are not mandatory? Who are the best subordinates? Who are the weakest subordinates? How can I stack the deck for success?

Here is the crucial part of creating a plan—the "what ifs." The smart leader should always think through the "what ifs" and have a plan on how to handle them before they occur. Time so spent is never wasted. Things do not always go as planned. If even only one "what if" comes to pass, the leader will be ready and ahead of the game. In combat zones, while creating a plan for an operation or even after it kicked off, I always thought through the "what ifs" and had my operations and intelligence officers do the same. The best leaders in any enterprise see problems coming and stack the deck to prevent negative "what ifs" from happening. They also have contingency plans to take advantage of positive openings which occur in fleeting windows of time.

The smart leader must also be mindful of his organization's constraints and center of gravity. There can be one or several constraints that inhibit getting the job done. In my time as a commander, there were always constraints to deal with—whether in battle in Korea or Vietnam, as an infantry division commander, as an Army Training Center commander in California, even as Executive Vice President of a major ski resort in Colorado. Constraints are normal. How they are dealt with is leadership.

First, the constraints must accurately be identified. If money and funding were short, the first area I looked into was infrastructure. Was it out of balance? Too big? Too small? Improperly organized for the expected output? What does each activity cost? I've found that in life, most decisions come down to two primary considerations: timing and money. And, how they are dealt with involves judgment, which I will get into later.

Here are some examples of the many constraints I've dealt with:

- **In Korea and Vietnam, my units were never up to strength. In my companies in Korea, I also had soldiers who spoke only Spanish (Colombian UN attaches) or Korean (ROK soldiers).**

- **In the Battle of Ia Drang, I went into that fight short almost 300 men. I also had only sixteen Huey helicopters to shuttle small groups into the landing zone from fourteen miles away.**

- **In my Infantry Division in Korea, 1970–71, race relations and drug abuse were the toughest of the many significant constraints.**

The "center of gravity" is the principal thing or activity that must be in balance or under control for an organization to operate; it is the organization's source of strength. In addition to understanding your own center of gravity to protect it, you must recognize and attack your enemy's or competitor's center of gravity to defeat them. In that battle in Vietnam, my center of gravity was the Landing Zone. I had to keep that lifeline open for ammo, water, and medical evacuation. If it fell into enemy hands…disaster. At Fort Ord, my vital center of gravity was keeping my hundreds of Drill Sergeants effective, well-trained, and in high morale. As commander of the Army Personnel Center for sixteen months, and Personnel Chief of the Army for two-and-a-half years, I had two mutually-supporting centers of gravity: (1) Meeting recruiting goals and (2) rebuilding an NCO Corps destroyed by the Vietnam War.

While getting the job done, the leader must plan ahead and create the future. He must be proactive, not reactive. Truly great leaders have acuity, are perceptive, aggressive, enthusiastic, can see the trends, analyze them carefully and correctly, have a vision, have confidence in it—and can inspire and motivate himself and his people to make it happen. He must have a positive attitude and must hate the word "No." He must have smart, well-trained people to run day-to-day activities. He must check up on them and make sure the job is getting done while he stacks the deck for future success.

Principle #3: "When nothing is wrong, there's nothing wrong—EXCEPT there's nothing wrong. That's when a leader has to be the most alert."

Complacency kills. Leaders are paid to create order out of chaos.

History is replete with examples of leaders who failed because they became too complacent. In the days and months leading up to Pearl Harbor, American military leaders were confident that the Japanese could never strike American soil. Our Naval Intelligence said that Pearl Harbor was too far out of reach for a Japanese naval task force. They were also convinced the harbor was too shallow for a torpedo attack. Instead of prioritizing the threat from an aggressive naval enemy, the Army Air Corps commanders at Wheeler and Hickam Fields put a higher priority on the threat from spies and saboteurs. They grouped the planes together at the airfield to make them easier for walking sentries to guard on foot patrol. But when the Japanese bombers arrived on December 7, the clustered American planes became "turkey shoot" targets.

In January 1968, the war in Vietnam was going well despite the backlash at home and the gross mismanagement from Washington. We were ahead in the body count and we hadn't lost a single battle. The North Vietnamese had called a cease-fire to observe the holiday known as "Tet"—the Vietnamese New Year. However, the Viet Cong and North Vietnamese had no intention of abiding by the cease-fire…and we were foolish to think they would. Under the cover of this "cease-fire," the Viet Cong launched a coordinated attack on critical US and South Vietnamese installations.

Although we were unprepared for the Tet Offensive, our forces crushed the Viet Cong uprising. In fact, it was a resounding defeat for the communists. But the American media painted a very different picture. Television broadcasts showed the Viet Cong storming the American Embassy in Saigon. Days later, CBS News anchor Walter Cronkite declared the war was now "unwinnable" and public opinion never recovered. We let our guard down, we underestimated the enemy, and we let the media spin the truth. The resulting crisis of confidence sabotaged our success.

Principle #4: "Trust Your Instincts."

Instincts are the product of one's personality, experience, reading, and education. Some call it "intuition" or "a gut feeling." It is kind of a sixth sense. When seconds count, instincts and decisiveness come into play. In quick-developing situations, the leader must act fast, impart confidence to all around him, must not second guess a decision—MAKE IT HAPPEN! In the process, he cannot stand around slack-jawed when he's hit with the unexpected. He must face up to the facts, deal with them, and move on. When my head tells me to do one thing, and my gut tells me to do another, I always go with my gut. Why? Because my gut, as I've learned, is rarely wrong.

Instinct is kind of a caution light, an early warning, or a gut feeling which can on occasion result in a far better decision than one based on a logical process. One rule of thumb that I learned more than sixty years ago at West Point is: "If there's doubt in your mind, there's no doubt at all." In other words, if you know in your heart that an action is wrong, *don't do it*. One of my sons calls this "The Rule of Doubts." Above all, never try to fake out, deceive, or fool the people under you. Not only is it wrong, but the troops can smell BS from miles away.

When a quick decision is not required, I get all the information, look into the pros and cons, and then back off from it using two approaches. One approach is to reach a tentative decision at day's end. Do not announce it. Instead "sleep on it" during the night and reconsider it early the next morning when your brain is fresh. The other approach is to move around—go to the gym for a workout, or take a run to get your blood moving faster. I am not medically qualified to know why, but new ideas and thoughts hit me whenever I do that. Sometimes, the solution just pops into my head when I'm considering something else that may or may not be related to the issue in question.

Here is an example of my principles and values in action: Cyril R. (Rick) Rescorla, a decorated Vietnam veteran was Vice President for Corporate Security at Morgan Stanley Dean Witter in Building #2, the South Tower of the World Trade Center on September 11, 2001. I knew Rick very well. We served together in the 1st Cavalry Division in the historic Ia Drang Battle of November 1965 and in other engagements in Vietnam. He was the best Infantry platoon leader in battle that I served with in Korea and Vietnam.

Rick was born in Hayle, Cornwall, England on May 27, 1939. In 1943, before the Normandy invasion, Rick's hometown served as the headquarters of the 175th Infantry Regiment, 29th US Infantry Division. He grew up idolizing the American GIs stationed in his hometown, and remarked to his mother that he wanted to be a soldier. Rick fulfilled his dream initially by joining the British Army in 1956, where he served as a paratrooper during the Cyprus insurgency. After a stint with the Northern Rhodesia Police (then a British protectorate), Rick came to America and enlisted in the US Army in 1964. After his service in Vietnam, Rick earned a law degree from Oklahoma City University. Meanwhile, he stayed in the Army Reserve and retired as a Colonel. In 1997, he was diagnosed with inoperable cancer and only six months to live. He would have none of that. He fought back, beat the odds, and sent the disease into remission (*Three strikes and you're not out*).

On September 11 at 8:48 a.m. when the first hijacked jet flew into the North Tower, the loud speakers in the South Tower came alive blaring "Do not leave the building. This area is secure." Rick disagreed. He had, before 9/11, conducted periodic evacuation rehearsals of the 2700 Morgan Stanley employees—from the President on down. (*There's always one more thing you can do*). He immediately ordered the evacuation of all 2,700 Morgan Stanley people out of WTC Building 2 (44th through 74th Floors) and 1,000 others out of WTC Building 5 close by—against instructions from a Port Authority official. (*When there's nothing wrong, there's nothing wrong except there's nothing wrong*).

At 9:07 a.m. eighteen minutes after the first strike on Tower 1, the second hijacked plane slammed into the South Tower. By then, hundreds of the Morgan Stanley employees were out of the South Tower and Building 5 and the rest were on the way. (*Trust your instincts*). Rick's instincts to get his people out of danger were right on.

The South Tower went dark, fires broke out, windows exploded. Rick was seen on several floors (as high as the 72nd) hustling people out, including disabled persons. Survivors reported seeing him on the 10th floor or the ground floor before the South Tower collapsed. When last observed, he was headed back up to make sure stragglers were out of there. He was never seen again. Rick's preparations for a possible disaster, his instincts, his decisiveness, and his personal actions in that terrible crisis—calm as always—saved hundreds of lives. He and five others were lost.

Throughout this book, you will see more instances of the Four Basic Principles in action. But whether your goal is to win the battle, close the sale, serve the public interest, or score the winning touchdown, these principles will help guide you—the leader—to success.

SUMMARY: THE FOUR BASIC PRINCIPLES

Principle #1: Three strikes and you're not out.

Principle #2: There's always one more thing you can do to influence any situation in your favor. And after that, there's one more thing.

Principle #3: "When nothing is wrong, there's nothing wrong – EXCEPT there's nothing wrong. That's when a leader has to be the most alert."

Principle #4: "Trust Your Instincts."

CALL OF DUTY

On November 14, 1965 at 2:30 in the afternoon, Senior Lieutenant Colonel Nguyen Huu An, of the People's Army of Vietnam, and I were doing our best to kill each other. We'd been at it for 2 hours in the miserably hot, humid scrub jungle fringing a football field-sized clearing in the remote Ia Drang Valley of South Vietnam. He was commanding well-trained, well-armed soldiers of the 66th North Vietnamese Regiment. I was a Lieutenant Colonel, an infantry paratrooper, commanding a 450-man Air Assault Infantry Battalion. The problem for me, at that moment, was that I'd only been able to bring in about 250 of my men. I had sixteen Huey helicopters and it was a 20-minute round trip from the pick-up/loading areas. Lt. Col. An was attacking with upwards of 1,800 very aggressive soldiers fiercely determined to kill us all. I was suffering heavy casualties, both killed and wounded, among my troopers. We were in a struggle for survival in the first major battle between US Army and North Vietnamese regulars.

The thought quickly crossed my mind that, however it turned out, many major military and political decisions would be made on both sides. But never once did it cross my mind during that 3-day battle that we would go down. I *knew* we would prevail.

More on that in a later chapter. For now, where was the starting point that landed me on that far field in Asia?"

Where, indeed?

The story of Harold Gregory Moore, Jr. begins in the foothills of the Ohio River Valley. Born on February 13, 1922 in Bardstown, Kentucky,

"Hal" was the eldest of four children born to Harold Sr. and Mary Moore (nee Crume). At the time of Moore's birth, Bardstown was a small wisp of a community numbering less than 4,000 in population. As Moore described it, Bardstown was "perfect, small, and caring...where parenting was made easier by the strong sense of community, Almighty God, and the shared love of all who chose to make it their home. Walking down Main Street as a boy was always a 'family' event as everyone knew everyone." In many ways, Hal Moore was also a product of his time. His was the generation that grew up hearing the harrowing tales of the Great War, the decadence of the Roaring Twenties, and experiencing the hardships of the Great Depression.

Despite the economic turmoil, however, the Moore family fared better than most. Even during the darkest days of the Depression, Moore recalled, "My father had good work, and there was always plenty to eat." Still, life for Moore and his three siblings—Betty, Bill, and Ballard—centered on the daily disciplines of work and Catholic piety. "All youth are somewhat shaped by their surroundings," he said, "as was I." From this foundation, Hal Moore drew his first lesson in leadership:

The discipline that makes an effective leader begins in the home.

"In most cases," he continues, "learning comes through observation and experience. It is through the parents and/or legal guardians where we first begin to understand right from wrong, and success or failure. In having guidelines and expectations set before me as a young boy, having to 'toe the line' was the standard of every day. While I remember my mother and father requiring discipline and proper conduct, there was an equal balance of love, fun, fishing, reading, religion and daydreaming. Yes, daydreaming."

Moore's childhood, in fact, fit the image of most young boys growing up in small-town America. While immersing himself in the local variety of team sports—football, baseball, and basketball—he took odd jobs in the community to appreciate the value of hard work and to earn a dollar. "I cut grass for a number people, was a water boy at the Guthrie Distillery Warehouse, and I caddied at the local golf course." This was a time in America when men roamed from town to town looking for any means of employment they could find. It was not uncommon for itinerant workers (victims of the Great Depression) to show up in a strange town and go door-to-door, asking residents to cut lawns, prune gardens, or chop wood in exchange for a meal or a few cents of pocket change. For Hal

Moore, finding and executing these jobs within the community taught him another valuable lesson:

No job is ever "beneath" you. In whatever you do, do it to the best of your abilities.

This powerful work ethic was essential to living in the Moore household. Indeed, every member was expected to contribute to the family's welfare. "I remember having to do family chores by chopping kindling and bringing in the coal for the stoves and fireplaces, being read to and reading, having to be respectful to adults and others, being comfortable in being alone, wanting my parents to be proud of me, having to share food on the table, having to sit and stand up straight, appreciating my childhood friends, fishing with my father, the structure imposed by my parents, learning that daily life was not all about me, how my parents would take time to listen to me, my parents giving me a special smile and how that made me feel, and having to help an elderly person who needed help at their home."

These tenets were reinforced by the family's devotion to the Catholic faith. "It was most important in our family to believe in God," Moore says. "My parents were daily practicing followers of Christ and we children were taught the same. Dad was Catholic, and Mother was Methodist." Yet Harold and Mary's denominational differences never disrupted their marriage. In fact, as Hal recalled, "she was more Catholic in some of her ways, as she would go to church and light candles for our family all of her life." By all accounts, Mary was the family's emotional bedrock. "There was an air of grace created mostly by my mother," Moore recalls, "that I can still feel today. She was an amazing woman. If there was ever an example of God working in our family, she was it. God chose her. The rest of us would live our lives trying to follow in her favored and saintly footsteps."

"She also taught herself how to play the piano and was a member of the local dance band. Often, we gathered around the piano and we would sing along. Mother became the model for future women in my life, and Dad became the faithful and loyal model for future mentors—and for me as a future father."

"We were not a perfect family," he admitted, "but we were 'FAMILY' through thick and thin. Yes, I do understand one thing—times are tough and parenting is perhaps far more challenging today than ever before. As I turn over every leaf in thinking through the years of my youth, there was one common building block practiced by my parents, day in and day out, in good times or bad. They brought to parenting a strong moral compass, something I hope was passed on to a young, maturing boy who tried to understand." From this, Moore internalized another important leadership lesson:

The best leaders strive to create a "family environment" within their organization.

A good leader aims to make his subordinates feel that they are valued members of a team. The same loyalty that goes "up" the chain-of-command must also go "down" the chain-of-command, and "across" the network of subordinates. The highly-functioning subordinates are the ones who feel that the leadership is fair and that their teammates "have their back."

These formative years in Bardstown during the Great Depression were, as Moore described them, "days of shaping and guidance, being challenged and accepted, and in subtle ways, beginning to learn the art of leadership. Those were the days of learning to lead oneself. I learned early in life that:

The first person you have to lead and discipline is yourself.

Good vs. poor choices make all the difference in the world. Within the family and in elementary school, obedience mattered. My early school days, taught by nuns of The Sisters of Charity, reinforced what I was experiencing at home. Bethlehem Academy had its priorities right: God, family, and school. I never forgot the order of those three foundational rocks in my young life. And if I did, Mom and Dad would set me straight fast."

Still, Moore was in many ways a typical teenager. "During my teenage years," he said, "I attended St. Joseph's Preparatory boarding high school—for boys only—in Bardstown, as a day student—we were called 'Day Hops.' It was a continuing path of obedience and shaping of my character. Like others, I had my fair share of conduct issues and I was punished for troubles I got into. A ruler over the head, or on the palm of a hand, by the Brothers of St. Xavier always seemed to redirect my focus to becoming more obedient and respectful.

"I loved team sports—baseball, football, and being physically fit. I never accomplished much in sports but I did have a strong will to be physically and mentally fit. We were often able to mix with the girls' high school for special events, which I did enjoy. During these four years, though, I was at war with myself. One part of me wanted to excel with others and another part of me wished to be alone, in the quiet and to further my relationship with God. These were times that caused considerable internal strife. I am confident all teenagers experience similar challenges in their growing years, but if that was the case back then, we never really talked about it."

Still, during these formative years, Moore was most comfortable dancing to the beat of his own drum. "In the early years of being a teenager," he said, "I loved fitting in, but there was something different in me. Later on, I learned the difference was that I followed my own path. It was never my instinct to follow others just because others had been there before me. It was exciting to be this way." Unlike most teenagers of his day, Hal had a voracious appetite for reading and took a keen interest in all things military. Indeed, when he wasn't riding his bicycle, casting lines at the local fishing hole, or taking care of his younger siblings, Moore could be found at the Bardstown Public Library, devouring any book he could find on military history. "I found very special opportunities to grow," he said. "I developed a love for reading and recall the school librarian jokingly saying to me, 'I believe you have read almost every book in the library.' My particular interests seemed to be with history, and non-fiction works from the great leaders of the world." He particularly enjoyed reading about the battlefield commanders of the American Revolution and the Civil War. From George Washington to Winfield Scott, these men embodied the same values which Moore sought to keep in his own life. And by the dawn of his teenage years, Hal knew that he had found his calling. His thirst for knowledge highlighted another key lesson in leadership philosophy:

To be a leader, you must be willing to be a lifelong learner.

The leaders who fail are those who think they know everything—or that they have nothing left to learn. They resent having to learn something new or adapt to a new situation. For a leader, "learning" does not strictly mean gaining new technical knowledge or refining a skill set. It means gaining an understanding of how to manage people in ways that maintain their trust and loyalty while preserving their dignity. It also means learning ways to maximize a team's strength while minimizing their weaknesses.

It means learning how to improve processes that maximize outputs while maximizing individual talents—all while inspiring subordinates in an atmosphere of respect rather than fear.

Moore also realized that a good leader is also a *good listener.* "I like to do a lot of listening," he said, "that way I pick up a lot of good ideas—many from subordinates. When you listen, you know twice as much as the other guy: what he knows and what you know. Also, whenever the boss talked, I not only listened but I took notes. I still carry 3x5 cards today."

His son, Steve, recalls the advice Moore gave him upon Steve's entry into active duty. "Before reporting into the 7th Infantry Division in 1975, I wanted to sit down with Dad and get his perspective on how to be a good officer. I broke out a few beers and expected a long conversation, but the advice was short and sweet. 'Keep your mouth shut and *listen* to your NCOs.' The discussion moved on to a more complicated topic... fishing."

"When I was 15 years old," Hal said, "I had given no thought to the future beyond the next football, basketball, or baseball game I'd be involved in. But my father gave thought to the future. He was a life insurance agent— no savings, a father of four, and never finished high school. Neither had my mother."

"My father had a dream. He wanted each of us kids to get a college degree. Somehow, some way, he would make it happen – or influence it to happen. He called me to his office in the spring of 1937, before the world exploded into World War II, sat me down, and suggested I should try to get into the U.S. Military Academy at West Point and become an Army officer. That became my dream, my goal."

Indeed, Hal was enthralled by West Point's legacy of leadership. Its graduates included many of the heroic leaders whom he had read about at the local library—including Ulysses S. Grant, Robert E. Lee, and Stonewall Jackson. Since its founding in 1802, West Point had been the nation's premier military academy and the primary source of commissioned officers for the US Army. The school was renowned for its uncompromising standards of honor and discipline—and the famed gothic architecture of the campus complemented its reputation as one of the most rigorous schools in America.

Gaining admission to West Point, however, was no easy task. The applicant files read like a "Who's Who" of America's best young scholars. Admission to the Academy was further restricted by a Congressional nomination process. A prospective cadet first had to obtain a nomination from his Congressman or Senator to be considered for admission. Moore certainly had the academic credentials, but he knew that his chances of receiving a nomination from the "backwoods of Kentucky" were slim to none.

Opportunity knocked on the afternoon of February 12, 1940. "It was my senior year in high school," he says. "I was offered a job by the Kentucky Senator Albert Benjamin 'Happy' Chandler in the Senate Book Warehouse in Washington, D.C. making $30.00 a week. My Dad had worked on his behalf in the election campaigns. I left home the next day thinking I'd have a good chance of finding an appointment to the Military Academy while in Washington right under the noses of every Senator and Congressman. I rented a room and finished high school at night in June 1940 with middle-aged cab drivers and government workers." His job in the Senate Book Warehouse consisted mostly of clerical tasks—inventorying, stocking, and shipping various titles. Mundane and repetitive as the job was, Moore embraced it with delighted enthusiasm. Every day, he rose from his bed in the hopes that he would find a Congressman or Senator with an unfilled appointment to West Point. "Periodically, the Army published a list of Congressmen and Senators who still had West Point appointments unfilled. The Senate Warehouse was close to the House and Senate office buildings. I knocked on doors, and asked for appointments. No luck for two and a half years." In the meantime, he enrolled at George Washington University in the fall of 1940. Moving out of his rented room, he pledged membership to the Kappa Sigma fraternity and eventually became their house manager. Although Moore had not yet received his appointment to the Academy, he vowed to remain in Washington until he did.

Ironically, his fortunes changed on December 7, 1941. Early that morning, the Imperial Japanese Navy launched a surprise attack on Pearl Harbor. "I was shocked like everyone else in America," Moore says. "No one had anticipated a first strike against Hawaii, much less from the Japanese. The following day, the US declared war on the Axis Powers." The next spring, "Congress doubled the numbers of cadets and midshipmen to the nation's service academies. I went into high gear visiting Congressional offices. *Again, no luck*. However, my own Congressman—Ed Creal, from the 4th District of Kentucky—said he would appoint me to the Naval Academy at Annapolis, Maryland. I thanked him very graciously and respectfully. I asked if he would appoint another Congressman's applicant to Annapolis if that Congressman would appoint me to West Point. That set him back. Mr. Creal was surprised, *but* he agreed to such a swap. Then,

I went into overdrive and found Congressman Eugene E. Cox of Georgia who agreed to the deal. He appointed me to West Point. I received a telegram from the War Department to report to the Military Academy on July 15, 1942."

Reflecting on this "horse trade" to get into the Academy, Moore internalized the following observations:

- **You've got to have a dream to move towards, or you're dead in the water. Once you've realized that dream and accomplished that goal—get another!**

- **I could create the future. I *could* make my dream happen.**

- **Never say "No" to yourself when you need to ask for something. Make the other guy say "No."**

- **Never quit! When you take a big hit, get back up. It's a lot easier to go down than to crawl back up when your morale is down. JUST DO IT! You can control your will to win.**

- **Find a way to turn every "minus" into a "plus"—like that Annapolis appointment; to me it was a "minus" I turned into a "plus."**

- **There *is* a solution to every problem; some are more complex than others. There's *always* a way.**

- **I could handle all my expenses on a small amount of money without outside help. Leaders are often faced with the arduous task of "doing more with less."**

In the summer of 1942, Moore's incoming class was the largest in West Point's history. The cadets' first day at West Point was known as Reception Day, or "R-Day." It marked the beginning of a strenuous indoctrination known as Cadet Basic Training, or "Beast Barracks," as it was commonly known. Although exclusively for West Point cadets, Beast Barracks resembled the Basic Training program of the Regular Army. Most West Point graduates remember their R-Day as a blur of savage put-downs, dreadful stares, close calls with heat exhaustion, and the constant reminder that "I *wanted* to come to West Point." For Hal Moore, R-Day certainly lived up to its chaotic reputation.

"No West Pointer can ever forget his arrival at that place."

Reflecting on his arrival at the rockbound citadel, Moore recalled an inspirational verse whose author remains unknown:

The determinate West Point that is to be his master for four years and the shaper of his destiny meets him at the top of the slope with ominous silence. He hears no voice, he sees no portentous figure; but there is communicated in some way, through some medium, the presence of an invisible authority, cold, inexorable and relentless. Time never wears away this first feeling; it comes back to every graduate on returning to West Point, let his years and his honors be what they may.

"And so it was for me," he says, "and still is."

"When the group of new cadets I was in arrived at the train station, we were met by a stone-faced, squared-jawed, multi-striped NCO with a pencil-thin moustache. His name fit him just as well as his spit-shined cavalry boots and riding breeches: Master Sergeant Bonebrake. He spent little time sizing us up, and I could tell that we didn't impress him for one minute. Bonebrake proceeded to march us up the hill to the gates of West Point—and there we were; on all sides, imposing gray buildings constructed of massive, rectangular granite blocks. Dead silence. But there was something else. It struck me then and to this day has always given me pause when I visit West Point; there's a certain majesty to the place, a sense of ageless permanence and a strong aura of powerful, unbending, no-nonsense authority. It was a powerful environmental shock to this 20-year-old. And there were more to come. Master Sergeant Bonebrake disappeared and handed us over to the 'Beast Detail.'

"An arriving appointee was not yet a Cadet. For mail purposes, he was a 'New Cadet.' When spoken to, he was addressed as 'Mister'—often Mister 'Dumbsquat,' 'Dumbjohn,' 'Dumbwilly,' or on rare occasions, his last name. For the next two months, he was given 'Cadet Basic Training.' We were instructed by upperclassmen; immaculately uniformed, ramrod erect, stern and unsmiling. We were formed into squads of eight men led by an upperclassman on the 'Beast Detail.' Our very first class was on the West Point Honor Code—'*A Cadet does not lie, cheat, or steal; nor tolerate those who do.*' After that, came Drill Instruction on marching in ranks, facing movements, and saluting. That afternoon, we marched onto the famous 'Plain'—the parade field at West Point—where we raised our right hands and swore an oath to follow and defend the Constitution of the United States of America."

It was here at West Point that Moore had his first sustained look at *toxic leadership*. "Each squad had two different squad leaders," he recalled— "one month with each." Both squad leaders would have a lasting impact on Hal Moore's style of leadership. "I have never forgotten those two men. The first was an arrogant, sadistic person who screamed and yelled at us, made us do unmerciful physical exercises, apparently with the goal of driving the weak to quit the Academy. I despised that man."

For as long as humans have been on Earth, every organization has had toxic leaders. They come in all shapes and sizes. A toxic leader will not always fit the mold of a stereotypical shouting martinet. Sometimes, toxic leaders take the form of a passive-aggressive liar or a disconnected, uninspiring "task manager." Throughout your life, you will probably serve under more bad leaders than good leaders. The irony, however, is that you can learn as much from a bad leader as you can from a good leader. Toxic leaders will set a perfect example of what not to be.

A leader should never be arrogant, spiteful, condescending, or engage in gossip. To the contrary, he should always act with humility and treat his subordinates with respect and dignity. As a leader, your words and actions have a greater impact on your subordinates than you realize. *Thus, choose your words carefully*. Avoid sarcasm and flippancy. Do not insult or take digs at anyone's intelligence. Remember, everyone processes information differently (and at different speeds). Don't automatically assume that someone is stupid or indifferent because they haven't mastered a particular task yet.

Contrary to popular belief, yelling at and berating your subordinates will not make them move faster nor will it inspire their loyalty. In fact, it may encourage them to begin plotting your demise. Many years from now, your subordinates will not remember what deadlines were met, what sales were closed, what products were shipped, or what training schedules were executed. What they will remember is how *you*, the leader, treated them—whether you inspired a climate of trust and dignity, or you ruled through fear, metrics, and intimidation. Some may think that toxic leadership is acceptable so long as the mission is accomplished. To be sure, completing the mission is important, but it should never come at the cost of trampling your subordinates' dignity or betraying their trust. Also, *talent is not a crutch for toxic leadership*. However talented you may be, you are *not* irreplaceable as a leader. There is always someone just as talented (or more so) than you.

During his time at West Point, Moore drew inspiration from a monologue titled: "Schofield's Definition of Discipline." A part of West Point's lore (and knowledge every cadet was required to memorize verbatim), this "Definition of Discipline" came from a speech delivered to the Corps of Cadets in 1879 by Major General John Schofield of Civil War fame. Schofield himself was a West Point graduate. It reads:

The discipline which makes the soldiers of a free country reliable in battle is not to be gained by harsh or tyrannical treatment. On the contrary, such treatment is far more likely to destroy than to make an army. It is possible to impart instructions and to give commands in such a manner and in such a tone of voice as to inspire in the soldier no feeling but an intense desire to obey, while the opposite manner and tone of voice cannot fail to excite strong resentment and a desire to disobey. The one mode or other of dealing with subordinates springs from a corresponding spirit in the breast of the commander. He who feels the respect which is due others cannot fail to inspire in them regard for himself; while he who feels, and hence manifests, disrespect toward others, especially his inferiors, cannot fail to inspire hatred against himself.

For as often as Moore was forced to recite Schofield's Definition of Discipline, he found it ironic that cadets like his first squad leader failed to heed it. That first squad leader, whom Moore characterized as a hateful man, represented just one strand of toxic leadership. Learning to identify toxic leaders is the first step in dealing with them. The various brands of toxic leaders include:

- Bully Leaders – those who inflict emotional pain, deliver threats and ultimatums, hurl insults, and invalidate the opinions of others.

- Narcissistic Leaders – those who are arrogant and self-congratulatory. This brand of toxic leader will often contrast his own abilities against a subordinate's shortcomings. "Look at me, I can do this so easily. Why can't you?" The Narcissistic Leader overbearingly forces himself and his personality onto the organization. He also presumes that he is the standard they should all strive to emulate. However, his tactics are so heavy-handed and self-aggrandizing that he inevitably earns the contempt of his subordinates.

- Divisive Leaders – He has many of the same qualities as the Narcissistic Leader, but he channels his wrath and arrogance towards one person (or a group of people) whom he perceives as weak or otherwise unfit to be a member(s) of the team. The Divisive Leader often resorts to public humiliation of the targeted individual(s) and builds a network of resentment and ridicule against that individual(s) until they leave the organization or are ousted by other means.

- Insular Leaders – This brand of leader forms cliques and goes to great lengths to ensure that his "followers" are shielded and enjoy special privileges. Meanwhile, those outside the leader's circle become targets for ridicule and derision. The "outsiders" are held to rigidly high standards, while those inside the clique are held to lower standards and given "free passes" for any infractions.

- Hypocritical Leaders – These leaders live by the mantra: "Do as I say, not as I do"—and rarely practice what they preach. The Hypocritical Leader will hold subordinates to a high standard, but won't apply that same standard to himself. *This is a guaranteed formula for failure—both for the leader and his organization.* You, the leader, set the ethical climate for your subordinates. Don't presume to demand good behavior if you are unwilling to exhibit the same. A recent survey indicated that nearly 54% of corporate employees admitted to unethical behavior on the job. Yet these same respondents admitted to seeing similar behavior (or worse behavior) at the upper echelons of the company. Remember, a leader sets the ethical standards for his organization.

- Enforcement Leaders – This mid-level leader seeks the approval of his superiors without regard to his subordinate's welfare. He will consciously follow orders that are bad, unsafe, or illegal only to stay in the good graces of the organizational culture.

- Callous Leader – in a similar vein to the Enforcement Leader, the Callous Leader has a blatant disregard for his subordinates' welfare or desires. This disregard may not stem from a desire to please the boss, but it definitely stems from a lack of empathy. The Callous Leader, much like the Bully Leader, exhibits sociopathic behavior.

- Seniority Preference Leader – Unlike the Insular Leader, this leader may not form cliques but he will always give preferential treatment to those who have served the longest time within the organization. Seniority ought to be rewarded in some respects, but the Seniority Preference Leader will defer to the "old guard" even at the peril of the organization. This can (and often does) lead to bad behavior among senior members. Here is an illustrative example of the Seniority Preference Leader at work:

    An argument breaks out between a new hire and a senior employee. Both report the incident to their manager. The new hire tells the truth about the incident; the senior employee lies. The manager, however, accepts the senior employee's version, saying: "I'll believe a vested employee before I believe a new hire."

    As a leader, you should never give a subordinate the benefit of the doubt simply because of their rank or seniority. History is replete with examples of high-ranking, high-profile people whose offensive behavior led to their downfall. High rank, fancy titles, and time in service did not stop them from acting dishonorably.

- Credit-hog Leaders – These leaders show their toxicity by taking credit for an employee's success or contribution. They resent the notion of giving credit where it's due.

- Blame-shifting Leaders – The mirror image of the "Credit-hog" is the blame-shifter. This leader is quick to point the finger for anything that goes wrong and, many times, he proactively looks for someone to whom he can assign the blame. The blame-shifter will often maliciously accuse someone of wrongdoing without evidence or probable cause. For example, if the computer network goes down while you were using it, the blame-shifter says: "You must have broken it." If your car gets a flat tire, the blame-shifter says it must be your fault. According to the blame-shifter, there is no such thing as an accident or bad coincidence—everything is *somebody's* fault.

Moore's second squad leader, however—who took over the squad during the second month of Beast Barracks—was the exact opposite. Moore described him as "stern, demanding, and he allowed no second-rate performances in anything. He had a calm, commanding, and forceful personality. He required and got the best out of all of us. His very presence was projected around him. He placed great emphasis on the West Point Honor Code, carefully instructed us on the Honor System and the stern, unforgiving nature of its application to all aspects of daily life, athletics, academics, and its extension throughout our future lives as commissioned officers. He also explained to us the demands, duties, and honor of living up to the West Point motto: 'Duty, Honor, Country,' as a cadet and as a Regular Army Officer. His name was Hiram G. Fuller—Class of June, 1943." After graduation, Fuller became an Engineer Officer and deployed to the Pacific with the 98th Infantry Division. Fuller would later serve in Korea and Vietnam before retiring as a Colonel in 1969. He passed away in 1993. As Moore recalled, "He was an early and excellent role model."

For the young New Cadet Moore, Hiram G. Fuller exemplified many of the leader attributes needed for success—including willpower, competence, and disciplined initiative. *Will is the inner drive that compels a subordinate to keep going when it would be easier to quit.* Yet, without competence, willpower is meaningless. Your subordinates may be willing (and even eager) to do their jobs, but they must know *how* to do their jobs—and how to do them well. As former Army Chief of Staff Peter Schoomaker once remarked, "We must not mistake enthusiasm for capability."Thus, a leader's task is to develop their subordinates' *will* along with their *skill*.This begins with realistic training with consistent standards.

Initiative is often defined as the ability to be a "self-starter"—to act in the absence of orders. Initiative also enables leaders to take charge of a situation when everything devolves into chaos. Initiative drives you, the leader, to find better methods, anticipate what needs to be done, and to act without being told what to do. The leader must take care, however, not to make a hasty decision or take initiative just for the sake of taking initiative.

As a leader of any stripe, you cannot simply give orders and expect your subordinates to follow them blindly. To the contrary, you must establish a clear intent (addressing the "why") and the desired end state. It will never suffice for a leader to say "Because I said so" as a reason for performing tasks.

If you can't justify the rationale of an order to yourself, don't make your subordinates do it. Re-evaluate your reasons and find another method.

It's also important for a leader to remember that disciplined initiative does not appear on its own. It must be cultivated within your subordinates. You, the leader, can either develop initiative by encouraging independent thought within organizational guidelines, or you can stifle initiative through micro-management and refusing to consider alternate points of view.

Following Hiram Fuller's example, Moore also realized that a good leader cultivates a sense of duty within his subordinates. "Duty means selfless devotion. Duty is selfless because it requires sacrificing the 'me first' attitude and replacing it with a commitment to others—God, country, and family. Duty is like faith—duty is unwavering, never gives up, and lasts through every challenge and trial. It is duty that builds all the great things in life. How was America made? Through the duty of the Patriots to each other and to their cause of freedom. How is America made strong today? Through the duty of each of us to improve the lives of one another.

"Duty at work means completing the tasks assigned, and achieving results, without succumbing to distraction. It is common to let interruptions interfere with getting the job done on time and done well.

However, duty at work is shown by a focus on work and 'a sense of urgency' in completing tasks. In this manner, we allow others to finish their work better and show the selflessness that duty means."

While receiving his crash course in comparative leadership, however, Moore discovered that he genuinely enjoyed the military training. Throughout Beast Barracks, he immersed himself in the fundamentals of soldiering: rifle marksmanship, patrolling, hand grenades, and the proper technique of shining shoes. "By August, we had been to the firing range, run the obstacle course, taken the physical efficiency tests, learned to prepare a 40-pound pack with bedroll, and demonstrated skill in hand-to-hand combat." Moore remembered that the high point for him during Beast Barracks "was firing EXPERT on the M-1 rifle with the top score in the company and being given a pint of vanilla ice cream by my Squad Leader."

Beast Barracks culminated with the so-called "Plebe Maneuvers" at Pine Camp (present-day Fort Drum) near Watertown, New York. It was a weeklong field exercise which introduced cadets to the art of bivouacking and how to maneuver at the squad and platoon level. Upon their return to West Point, "we regrouped into new companies formed as the Corps grew from one to two regiments to accommodate our large class." Moore found himself assigned to Company C-1 (C Company, First Regiment). "Beast Barracks had come to an end. It was time to start the academic year."

Although Moore excelled in English and History, he perennially struggled in Math and the hard sciences. "My principal problem at West Point," he recalls, "centered on the mathematically-based Engineering subjects. Back then, our Bachelor of Science degree was awarded in 'Military Science and Engineering'—so the bulk of our courses were in higher-level math, engineering (civil, electrical, and, mechanical), physics, chemistry and the like. By the end of October 1942, my name was on the list of men who were found 'Deficient' in math. If I had continued to be 'Deficient,' I would have been discharged from the Military Academy at Christmas. I was severely frightened. After all my work getting into West Point, I was in danger of being kicked out. I was determined that would *not* happen."

"I was glued to my advanced math textbooks every night from 7:30 p.m. until lights out at 11:00 p.m.—and after lights out I moved to the nearby restroom down the hall from my room," where Moore sat on a toilet studying by the dim light of a 40-watt bulb. Plowing through his textbooks until 1:00 or 2:00 in the morning, he knew that even if "I didn't understand the advanced, arcane math and bewildering engineering, physics, and chemistry, I could at least memorize the procedures."

Moore made it through his first year at West Point by the skin of his teeth. It was, as he called it, "an academic trip from hell." He survived his midterms and finals, "but the distressing experience of struggling for weeks to get pro★ and stay pro—knowing the dire results if not, profoundly affected me. From then on, I led an unbalanced life at the Academy [i.e. few extracurricular activities and a lot of studying]."

In the midst of his academic turmoil, however, Moore did receive some unexpected good news: West Point's curriculum had been accelerated to three years instead of four. 'No longer were we the Class of 1946; we were now the new Class of 1945!' Moore later discovered that even though the curriculum had been shortened by a year, "the total hours of instruction actually increased."

Although he learned much about leadership and academic survival, Moore reflected that his first year at the Academy taught him more about himself than anything else. "I do wish to convey," he says, "that I have always believed each of us matures and comes into his own at different times of life. I can truthfully say that I do not think West Point made me. What West Point did do was *accurately pinpoint my strengths and weaknesses, and then helped me to become better and stronger in both*. In the areas of leadership courses and leadership roles, and with opportunities to rise within the student ranks at West Point, I met every possible challenge. However, to say that I became a top student in my class was just not the case. I was a middle-of-the-road cadet in almost every aspect of becoming a leader. I loved being there, but was always concerned about math courses and lived with much disappointment, especially during my plebe year.

"One special aspect of my life at West Point was the many relationships. The friendships were deep and caring...we began to learn and know that the person next to you would be there for you at all times. We started to realize we would die for the person next to us. That was something new and eye-opening. West Point was teaching us about the preciousness of life, and it was there where I began to understand what God expected of me."

Early during his West Point career, Moore found a safe haven in the Catholic Rectory. "The Catholic Chapel became a part of most days," he recalled. The Rector, Monsignor George Murdock, "became my friend and mentor. For the next three years, I attended Mass almost daily and

---

★ Cadet slang for "proficient."

helped with chores around the church in my little spare time. He was always there for me in the worst and best of times." Moore remembers it as being the most well-grounded aspect of his time at the Academy. "Remember what my parents preached—God, family, and school—in that order always."

Meanwhile, World War II raged on in Europe and the Pacific. Every Wednesday, Moore and his classmates had the opportunity to watch the latest *Staff Combat Film Report*, shown in the Chemistry Lab. "These vividly brought home what we were preparing ourselves to do. The scenes of fighting in both the Pacific and Europe gave us a contrast of environments as well as a better understanding of the enemies we would face." Sobering as they were, Hal knew that these films portrayed combat more realistically than any newspaper, radio, or movie newsreel. It also underscored an invaluable lesson in leadership:

Leaders stay informed of current events, and they should anticipate challenges based on those events.

But as Hal Moore entered his final year at West Point, the war was unmistakably winding down. The Class of 1944 had graduated on June 6—simultaneous with the D-Day landings in Europe. The cadets of '45 were thrilled to hear about the Normandy invasion, but "we wondered whether there would be any war left for us." Indeed, by the following spring, the Allies had penetrated deep into the Fatherland. With the Americans closing in from the west—and the Soviets from the east—a frantic Adolf Hitler committed suicide on April 30, 1945. One week later, the German Army surrendered and the news of V-E Day rang throughout the world. But even though the war in Europe had ended, the Japanese refused to quit the fight.

"In our last months at West Point in 1945, the First Classmen (college seniors) gathered in the big hall of the East Academic Building for 'Branch drawing.' Each cadet's name would be called out by his 'class standing'—and he would stand up and choose the branch to which he would be assigned at Graduation. Each would stand when his name was called and choose the Branch of Service to which he would be assigned. Each branch had a maximum number of slots and, when reached, the branch would be closed and not available to cadets with a lower class rank. The Engineer openings would be filled first (always), then Armor, Field Artillery…and last—the Infantry."

Branch selection was a nerve-racking experience for the young Cadet

Moore. During his three years at the Academy, he had labored away at his textbooks only to land in the bottom fifteen percent of his class. He desperately wanted to branch Infantry, but feared that the branch would fill its quota with the higher ranking cadets before he had a chance to make his selection. With bated breath, Moore heard each of his classmates call out their choice:

"Infantry!"

"Field Artillery!"

"Engineers!"

Fortunately, several infantry slots were still available when the announcer made his way down the list to "Moore, Harold G."

"When my name was called, only Coast Artillery and Infantry remained."

"Infantry!" – Moore cried out.

"Finally, June Week and Graduation and family and friends gathered to participate in its many events."* However, one of Moore's fellow cadets was nearly excluded from the company's end-of-year celebration. A week before graduation, the First Classmen in Moore's cadet company held a meeting to discuss plans for a company picnic. During that meeting, a few of Moore's classmates suggested that Cadet Ernie Davis and his family not be invited. "Davis was one of three black cadets at West Point in the early 1940s, and he was in the same Cadet Company I was in." Disgusted, Hal stood up and said that he would boycott the company picnic if Davis and his family were not invited. "Quickly, things were reversed and Davis and family attended with our other classmates and guests." His willingness to buck the trends of racial bigotry stands as another important lesson in leadership:

A good leader *never* discriminates or alienates based on race, color, or other genetic factors.

"On June 5, 1945, I graduated from West Point. General Omar Bradley handed me my diploma. *I did not consider myself a survivor; I was a winner.* I had defeated every challenge and never doubted that I would do so."

"Upon graduation, I made an internal assessment of my being the best possible leader I could be, no matter the situation. Was I ready? When looking in the mirror, I found the answer I needed: I must go back to my

---

* Cadet slang for the week of graduation, "June Week" offered a variety of parades, picnics, and activities for the families of the graduating cadets.

roots before my first orders were in hand."

"Thus, my roommate, James Herbert (who later became a Brigadier General), and I traveled to Kentucky and attended a silent three-day retreat at the Abbey of Gethsemane. I was 'home again with solitude' and had now completed what I might call an experience to be right with God. What I needed to be was the very best leader God intended me to be.

"I was about to travel my own path. I left West Point as 'below average' in class rank and in the lower levels of cadet leadership. That is a cold hard fact. But facing those facts as truth, I was determined to get better as a soldier every day."

Moore's Observations, Lessons Learned or Relearned:

- I learned to work efficiently and effectively under enormous pressure in a severely unforgiving, demanding environment.

- Self-confidence is a vital character trait. As I met and mastered new challenges, and successfully completed each year, every new victory increased my self-confidence—*a mandatory, essential character trait for a leader*. I learned that I must honestly *believe* I could accomplish anything.

- I was able to function mentally and physically, in top form, with only 5 – 6 hours of sleep a night.

- When I graduated, I did not consider myself a *survivor*. That's a negative. I was a WINNER. I had defeated every challenge.

- I don't remember the circumstances, but one of the self-leadership rules I learned at West Point is: "If there's doubt in your mind, there's no doubt at all".

- READ. I love to read books and have since a very young age. At West Point, I discovered a magnificent library loaded with books on military history and leadership. Ever since then, for more than sixty years now, I have been fascinated by the study of leadership—military, political, business, athletic, etc.—and within that, a focused interest in why leaders fail. Remember, a good leader is a life-long learner who continually studies to perfect his craft.

SUMMARY:

The discipline that makes an effective leader begins in the home.

No job is ever "beneath" you. In whatever you do, do it to the best of your abilities.

The best leaders strive to create a "family environment" within their organization.

If you can't justify the rationale of an order to yourself, don't make your subordinates do it. Re-evaluate your reasons and find another method.

Leaders stay informed of current events and they should anticipate challenges based on those events.

A good leader *never* discriminates or alienates based on race, color, or other genetic factors.

LEARNING THE ROPES

Hal Moore often said that "my military career began as World War II was ending." Indeed, by Graduation Day, Germany had surrendered, the Fürher was dead, and the Japanese were preparing to make their last stand in the Pacific. But as Americans celebrated V-E Day, the newly-commissioned Lieutenant Moore celebrated another victory. After three years of academic tribulation, he was proud to say that "I graduated at the top...*of the bottom fifteen percent of my class.*"

With Germany out of the war, the US sent more troops to the Pacific. Like many of his classmates, Hal received orders to report to the Far East Command. His first place of duty, however, would be the Infantry Officer Basic Course at Fort Benning, Georgia. After six weeks of tactical instruction, "I volunteered for the jump school (paratroop training) at Fort Benning." Unfortunately, "they only had openings for about twenty-five officers during that cycle, and a lot of my classmates also volunteered. They only took the top-ranking cadets, and I was not selected because I was way down at the bottom of my class." Disappointed, but not dejected, Hal Moore loaded his bags onto a train westbound for San Francisco— where a troop ship waited to take him to one of the many replacement depots scattered throughout the Pacific.

"The war in Europe was over," he said, "but we hoped to see action in the Pacific Theater." Sadly (or luckily), for Moore and his comrades, it was not to be. Following the nuclear devastation of Hiroshima and Nagasaki, the Japanese government finally lost its will to fight. On August 14, 1945, Emperor Hirohito announced his nation's unconditional surrender. He instructed all Imperial troops to lay down their arms and to cooperate with the newly-arriving occupation force. On September 2, in a ceremony held aboard the *USS Missouri*, a Japanese delegation signed the official document of surrender. World War II had come to an end.

Meanwhile, on the other side of the Pacific, the 23-year-old Lieutenant Moore boarded a troop ship in San Francisco Bay. Its destination, as he found out, was the Philippine Islands—to a replacement depot north of Manila. "We were disappointed that we had seen no combat duty." Still, the thought of going to war had been hauntingly real. "I personally knew upperclassmen who were killed in action," he said. "We were under no illusions about what we were headed for. I probably would have been killed jumping into Japan, because the entire Japanese population had been issued pitchforks to attack paratroopers."

After a two-week voyage, Moore disembarked at Manila Bay and settled into the replacement depot. It was nothing more than a "tent city," and Moore remembered that "I stayed there with a bunch of other second lieutenants from colleges all over the country." Because the war had ended, life at the depot was decidedly dull. "While there, I had the choice of waiting in the camp or taking limited travel on Luzon, the main island. I chose to travel. By hitching rides and walking, I visited the ravaged city of Manila, the abandoned and wrecked Clark Army Airfield, a Pygmy tribe deep in the jungle, some of the Bataan Peninsula Battlefields, and numerous other places."

One day, however, Moore and his friends were visited by a personnel officer taking volunteers for the various divisions assigned to occupation duty. Moore remembered that these units included the 24th Infantry Division, the Americal Division, and the 1st Cavalry Division, "but then I heard about the 11th Airborne Division," he said, "and that they had a jump school just north of Tokyo." Moore quickly volunteered and was on a plane to Tokyo the following morning.

Following the Japanese surrender, the 11th Airborne Division had been assigned to occupation duty on the northern half of Honshu (the main island) and on Hokkaido, the northernmost prefecture of the Japanese archipelago. After establishing its first command post at the Atsugi Airfield, the division parceled its Regiments into camps near the cities of Hakodate, Morioka, and Sapporo.

As Moore boarded the plane to Tokyo, he wondered how the Japanese would greet him and his fellow GIs. From the US newsreels and newspapers, he had learned of the atrocities carried out by the soldiers of the Rising Sun. Given the savagery of their conduct, many wondered if the Japanese intended to abide by the terms of surrender, or if a few "dead-enders" would continue to fight the Allied occupation.

Landing in Tokyo, however, Moore and his comrades discovered a hauntingly different picture: the Japanese *avoided* the Americans at all costs. Nevertheless, Moore admired the discipline and dignity with which they conducted their recovery efforts. "I was flown up to Japan in October [1945]... and was sent north on a train to Sendai for the 11th Airborne Division's Jump School. Arriving at the Tokyo Central Train Station, I was struck by the cleanliness of the place and by the hundreds of Japanese soldiers in uniform sitting on the floors, leaning against walls—all unarmed, no weapons—and showing no anger or antipathy towards the American soldiers. A Japanese rail conductor showed me to a spotless alcove with a short bunk and clean sheets. The train left on time and arrived in Sendai the next morning exactly on time. Here was my observation: these people were six weeks out of a five-year war and they had already begun cleaning up and disciplining their services. When they get back on their feet, watch out." Moore realized that:

Even in the midst of defeat, carry yourself professionally and maintain your discipline. That is the quickest way towards recovery.

Still, it was a different culture and not *every* Japanese citizen took well to the US occupation. Some would run in the opposite direction if approached by a US serviceman. One paratrooper also noticed that there were no women in sight. The few women that did sneak out into the daylight "had on baggy clothes to hide any female identification. Evidently, the Japanese expected us to come in raping and looting as they always did." Another of Moore's fellow paratroopers, WC Kitchen, remembered an incident where he was stopped by a Japanese officer and asked, 'Why don't you rape and loot and burn? We would.' Kitchen just looked at the man in disbelief. 'That man was genuinely puzzled by our actions,' he said. Yet, all Kitchen could say was: 'we just don't do things like that.'"

As a leader, you will inevitably have to interact with different cultures. You don't have to understand or agree with the mentality of a particular culture. However, you will have to operate within its framework and be aware of its dynamics. This is especially true during a post-war occupation or if you are being hosted by a foreign entity.

A good leader studies the culture of any location where he is planning to go—and he ensures his subordinates are properly educated on the same.

Following jump school, Moore received orders to report to the 187th Glider Infantry Regiment at Camp Crawford—just outside Sapporo, the prefectural capital of Hokkaido. It was November 1945 when he arrived at Regimental headquarters and was assigned to E Company, 1st Battalion. Meeting his platoon, Moore wondered if his new charges would take him seriously. Aside from a few replacements, they were all combat veterans, some of whom had been with the unit since its activation. They had been awarded Purple Hearts, Silver Stars, and bore the heralded wreaths of the Combat Infantryman Badge. And the fresh-faced Lieutenant Moore now had the monumental task of gaining their trust and respect. Nevertheless, Moore handled their first meeting with surprising ease. "Hello," he told them. "I'm your platoon leader. I'll do the best I can, and I expect the same from you." The meeting highlighted one of the most valuable lessons for a young leader:

When in charge, take charge, but treat your subordinates with respect, dignity, and common courtesy.

Being a leader does not mean that you are instantly the smartest person in the room. Everyone has unique talents and perspectives they bring to the organization. Therefore, a good leader utilizes the talents of those around him, seeks counsel from those with more experience, and treats others with respect. *Leaders sometimes forget that respect is two-way street: if you give respect, you get it in return.* This is simply a derivative of the Golden Rule: "Treat others how you want to be treated." Subordinates will respect a leader's rank and position, but they will not respect *him* unless he earns it through reciprocity. Some leaders adopt the mentality that "No one deserves respect until they earn it." Hal Moore's philosophy, however, was that *everyone* deserves respect until they did something to lose it. Recall the discussion in Chapter 2 regarding toxic leadership: failure to treat others with respect will lead to your demise as a leader.

Imagine if Moore had arrived at his platoon with an attitude of superiority and condescension. He would have failed miserably as an officer—especially since many of his subordinates were distinguished combat veterans. In the military and in civilian life, leaders often find themselves in positions where their subordinates have more experience and technical "know-how" than they do. Thus, condescending attitudes from the leader will only poison the workforce and undermine productivity. Remember this:

A worker's performance often reflects the attitude of his leadership.

Thus, if you treat your subordinates like dirt, that's exactly how they will perform: *like dirt.* You don't motivate people by insulting them. You don't inspire people by talking down to them. As a leader, you'd be surprised how easily you can motivate your subordinates with a little common courtesy. When setting the tone for your organization, consider the following rules of thumb:

- **If you want something done, ask nicely.**

- **If a subordinate forgets to perform a task, don't take it personally; just remind them nicely. In any organization, everyone has a "to-do" list. While juggling these tasks, some things will inevitably fall through the cracks. When that happens, don't assume that the subordinate is lazy or stupid. Simply re-engage them on the task and, if necessary, emphasize why it's a priority.**

- **If a subordinate performs a task and the outcome is not what you expected, don't attack their intelligence or their character. Politely explain the deficiencies and offer an idea for a solution. Subordinates quickly lose respect for any leader who is "all problem and no solution."**

"The leader," said Moore, "sets the *tone* and *attitude* of his people. Therefore, it's important to exude honesty, firm self-confidence, and unwavering commitment to be the best. Some people are born with that encoded, self-assured gene and are naturally confident in their abilities to shape the future, make the right decisions, and succeed. But it *can* be developed in others. The leader creates and enforces the standards of performance, institutional integrity, character and personality of his unit, his company, his team. As Arthur Newcomb said, 'Show me the leader and I will know his men. Show me the men and I will know their leader'"

Ultimately, Moore commanded his platoon for only three weeks. By the time he arrived at Camp Crawford, "there were very few captains," he said. "They were all being discharged." Indeed, most of the captains in Moore's unit were graduates of Officer Candidate School or had earned battlefield commissions. Thus, "after three weeks, I was suddenly a company commander! That was a great challenge for a second lieutenant with no combat experience and only five qualifying jumps."

Taking command of E Company, Moore noted that it was "woefully understrength and the draftees in the ranks [including the officers] who'd fought in the war were frequently leaving. We did receive a few replacement officers, but not many. Some companies had less than a hundred or so men. That's when I first learned the worth, the requirement, and the need for good intermediate leaders/supervisors/trainers over my troops in the ranks. In the military, these men are the Non-Commissioned Officers (NCOs). They were the leaders with 'street-smarts'—men who had spent years down with the troops while Commissioned Officers [lieutenants, captains, and the like] were moving between duties on staff, in schools, in higher headquarters, and (if lucky) in command positions. During my entire career, I consulted with and learned from NCOs."

Before joining the 11th Airborne Division, Moore admitted that "I had never heard of 'mentoring' but I now realize my first mentor was my Platoon Sergeant in E Company. He taught me so very much about soldiers in the ranks and soldiering. Throughout my career in the Army I consulted with and learned from NCOs—my First Sergeants, my Sergeants Major when I was a battalion, brigade, division commander—and the Sergeant Major of the Army when I was Personnel Chief of the Army." His chief observation, as he recalled, was this:

In business, the NCOs are the intermediate supervisors. The leader at the top should consult with and visit them frequently, on their turf, to learn more about what goes on down where the job gets done. It will help him make better decisions in future planning, and in assuring better performance. In the Army, the saying is: "An outfit does well the things the boss checks up on."

Although the post-World War II drawdown left the Regiment with few resources, Moore still found time to do his core competency training. "I did a lot of parachute jumping," Moore said, especially during the winter. "We did have training schedules to follow, but the deep snow and intense cold often inhibited that activity. Also, the exodus of men and Reserve Officers continued. Finally, spring [1946] came, the snow melted away, and the exodus slowed. We actually received some replacements."

Moore remembered it was an exciting time to be in the Army. By the spring of 1946, the Japanese no longer feared their American occupiers. However, the young GIs—excited the war was over and with little else to keep them busy—often ventured into town, got drunk, and took a strong liking to the Japanese brothels. Policing his soldiers "was a hell of a problem," Moore said, "because all they were interested in was drinking the Japanese beer and screwing the Japanese women." The Japanese had no societal hang-ups about sex—and the American GIs took full advantage of it. Several soldiers even had Japanese girlfriends in the local towns (many of whom returned to the US as war brides). Throughout 1946, it wasn't unusual for the Military Police to pick up a handful of GIs from a drunken caper, or for a soldier to miss his morning formation because he had overslept at the local brothel.

Nevertheless, Moore knew that many of his men were leaving the military and he didn't want to tie them up within the Army's legal system. Thus, whenever one of his troopers got picked up by the MPs, or took one too many romantic liaisons, Hal devised a simpler yet more creative way to punish them. "My punishment for them was to go running with me." Moore was an excellent runner and said, "I could run five to eight miles without breaking a sweat!" His punitive running routes would go around Camp Crawford and into the trails of the mountains surrounding the post. "And I would run these sons-of-bitches until they puked all over the ground." Any soldier who went for a punitive run with Hal Moore never made trouble for him again. By modern standards, this physical punishment may seem offensive, but it nonetheless underscores an important concept about disciplining subordinates:

Wherever possible, solve problems at the lowest level.

When leaders are confronted with disciplinary problems (be it willful disobedience, negligence, or honest mistakes), they must resolve these problems at the lowest level before raising the issue to higher echelons. If the problem can be fixed—and a remedy instituted—at the lower levels, it will benefit your relationship with your subordinates, improve the health of the organization, and not divert higher-level resources away from other priorities.

Imagine if Hal Moore had elected to turn one of his wayward GIs over to the Army legal system for prosecution. The soldier would have been removed from his duties (not good considering the unit was already understrength); then be incarcerated while awaiting formal charges and a court-martial (unnecessarily draining the Army's law enforcement assets);

and then go before a military judge to receive the prescribed punishment (delaying soldier's appointed date to exit the military and potentially hindering his prospects of post-war employment). Instead, Moore's "punitive runs" represented a simpler punishment that corrected the soldier's behavior, conserved higher-level resources for worse offenders, and did not disrupt the draftee's timeline for returning to civilian life.

These simple exercises in discipline taught Moore an even greater lesson in leadership:

⊗ Praise in public; punish in private.

As a leader, you should *never* resort to public humiliation when correcting a subordinate. It hurts unit cohesion and you may never regain that subordinate's trust or respect. "If you need to take someone to the wood shed," Moore opined, "do it in private."

"In the spring of 1947," Moore said, "I learned a very valuable lesson in the 'Social Graces'—a subject not taught to me at West Point. The port city of Otaru, on the Sea of Japan, was 30 miles west of Sapporo. A US Navy vessel had put into Otaru and the Commanding General of the 11th Airborne Division, Major General Joseph M. Swing, invited the naval officers and the officers of our Division to a reception at the Grand Hotel ballroom. I had never been to such an affair. It was a good party and we junior officers had a fine time. Food, drink, and good talk. But there was hell to pay.

"Early the next morning, all the West Point officers in the Division were ordered to report to the Commanding General in his office." Moore knew that this was *not* a good sign.

"Uh oh! We smelled trouble."

General Swing was a West Pointer—a member of the Class of 1915, also known as "The Class the Stars Fell On." Of the 164 graduates that year, 59 of them (36%) would achieve general rank—more than any other West Point class in history. Swing's classmates included Generals Dwight Eisenhower, Omar Bradley, and James Van Fleet (who later command the US Eighth Army during the Korean War). Swing, as Moore remembered, was a "handsome, hawk-nosed, steely-blue-eyed, six-foot, slim, few-words, no-nonsense general. His command presence radiated intensity."

As ordered, the West Point officers nervously assembled into Swing's office. "So, there we were," Moore said, "the full bird colonel commanding the 187th Regiment, the lieutenant colonels, and majors from the Division staff...and 10-12 green second lieutenants from the

West Point Class of '45."

General Swing wasted no time.

"He rose up from his desk and clumped out in front of us all as we stood at attention waiting for what we sensed would most certainly not be a happy occasion. With a cast (from a skiing accident) on one leg—which did not help his disposition—he just stood there grim, mean-eyed, saying nothing, riveting each of us in our eyes like an ice pick. Then he proceeded to lecture us on how West Point officers should set the example during such social occasions as the previous evening. He told us how grossly inhospitable we were to *his* guests in not socializing with the naval officers and making them feel welcome. He lectured us on how we all stood apart talking amongst ourselves, with other friends, enjoying the food and swilling down the drinks. I stood there, stark still at attention, eyes dead ahead. At one point, he raised his voice and strongly ordered: 'MOORE! LOOK AT ME!!' I did so instantly but wondered how the hell the General knew the names of even lowly second lieutenants!?

"After 10 minutes of it, General Swing said: 'Now, you will remember what I've told you for the rest of your lives, and you WILL so instruct your officers!!! DISMISSED!' Severely chastened, we quietly walked out, and went back to our duties." Moore later reflected that the lesson learned was obvious:

At an official reception, or dinner party, the real purpose of the event is to socialize, to talk with the other guests and participants—eating and drinking is secondary.

"The 11th Airborne had two of its Regiments in Northern Honshu (the large island of Japan) and the 187th on Hokkaido. The General had a *lot* of units to supervise, and he did so superbly."

"General Swing, a strong commander, put out the policy that all officers of his Division were NOT to fraternize with the Japanese women; any who did so would be sent back to America. Left unsaid was the fact it would be 'career ending.'" Of course, this directive didn't stop the young paratroops from engaging in liaisons with the femmes of Hokkaido. Hence, leaders like Moore meted out private punishments rather than risk livelihoods and disrupt unit readiness by reporting these "romantic infractions" up the chain of command.

"In mid-1946," Moore said, "the War Department began sending wives and children to join their husbands in Japan. Japanese homes were requisitioned in Sapporo for the few senior officer families. Soon, the demand grew to include family homes for lower ranks and for better barracks for the troops and for other necessary structures. General Swing was a troop-oriented commander; always concerned with not only their discipline and fighting ability but also for their welfare. As a consequence, the Army provided him the funds in early 1946 to build a camp—an Army base for the 187th Regiment, the Division Headquarters, and houses and barracks for its officers and men." After seven months as a company commander, Hal Moore suddenly found himself in charge of General Swing's construction project.

"There was a lieutenant colonel with the Army Corps of Engineers who was in charge of the money, plans, and supervision of building Camp Crawford. And when he rotated out, guess who became the new camp construction officer? Me. And I was responsible for $8,000,000!"★ It was an enormous responsibility for a young lieutenant. Hal Moore, with no experience in construction, had to finish what a lieutenant colonel had started in building a camp to house more than 4,000 individuals.

"My responsibilities were the construction of: barracks and dining halls for 2,700 troops; kitchens; living quarters and a dining hall for bachelor officers; a water treatment plant and water supply system; a sewage disposal plant and disposal piping; 210 residences for American families; seven boiler houses; facilities to steam heat all buildings; and 14 miles of paved roads with drainage systems."

Assessing the situation, Moore realized that: "I was an Infantry Lieutenant who had never broken the code at West Point on the cryptic, arcane mysteries of anything dealing with Engineering—except surveying. So, what did I do? I hired an excellent English-speaking Japanese interpreter to help me supervise the Japanese contractors. I pulled out my Engineering manuals, which began to make more and more sense as actual construction began and took form. I began to study spoken Japanese intensely and soon was able to understand and converse to a limited extent in that language, immersed as I was all day with the Contractors. It was fun!"

After the project's completion, General Swing was so impressed by Moore's work that he appointed him as the Post Engineer, responsible for overseeing the maintenance and repair of the camp's new infrastructure. "I did that job for a few months—still a lieutenant—until an Engineer Major took over and I went back to duty with the troops in E Company."

★ More than $103,000,000 in 2016 dollars.

Moore's Observations, Lessons Learned or Re-learned:

- Be confident, but not arrogant. Self-confidence and humility are the keys to getting any job done.

- There's always a way. Either you find a way, or you make one. If you can't think of a way, don't hesitate to ask for help. Take counsel from those who have the information and experience.

- Supervise. Check up on things but don't micromanage.

- <u>Make sure your subordinates understand their priorities of work.</u> Collaborate to streamline task lists so you can point quantifiable results by the end of the work day.

- Keep a positive attitude. Just do it.

Moore's return to E Company, however, was short-lived. Within weeks of his return from construction duty, he was appointed the Assistant Regimental Operations Officer. The new position put him under the direction of Major Herbert Mansfield. "He was the epitome of a 'Gung Ho' paratroop officer," Moore said—"blunt-spoken, charismatic, aggressive, a bit freewheeling, and devoted to duty and the Army. He had previously been commander of the Regiment's 1st Battalion based in Hakodate—250 miles south of Sapporo. I'd met him only once before when I was on a regimental inspection team checking company records. When we arrived, we were told that: 'Major Mansfield leads his battalion on a 4 mile run every morning at 6:00 a.m. and every man on his post participates—cooks, clerks, everyone—including all visitors AND every man carries his weapon. Visitors carry an issued rifle.' We ran with the troops. Later, in the Officer's Mess, when I walked in for breakfast, Major Mansfield invited me to sit at his table. My reply: 'Sir, I was headed over to eat with my friends." I had classmates in his battalion. His reply: 'We'll be your friends. Sit down.' I did.

"In the Army, lieutenants and captains are 'Company-Grade Officers;' majors, lieutenant colonels, and colonels are 'Field-Grade Officers.' One, two, three and four-star Generals are 'General Officers' or 'Flag Officers.' Lieutenants do not hob-nob with officers above them in rank. Now, suddenly and surprisingly, Major Mansfield had come down on me to be his assistant and the Regimental Commander OK'd it. It was great duty. When Mansfield gave me a task he would tell me clearly what he wanted, specify his standards, and then turn me loose—but, he would check on me now and again. He never told me *how* to do anything. In those first two years of the occupation, we were required to check on former Japanese airfields, camps, and ports to see if units had been disbanded, weapons turned in, etc. Thus, to keep up our airborne tactical skills, I conceived the idea of jumping a company into the site as if it were a combat operation. The troops loved it. I was also the Regimental Jumpmaster in charge of the periodic training jumps every soldier was required to make. I was in the Jump Door of every drop, responsible for deciding the exact moment for a 'stick' (10-12 men) to exit the C-47's Jump Door, considering wind, drop zone, location, aircraft speed, etc. I was also responsible for tactical jump training into the deep snow of Hokkaido in the winter—dropping skis and ammo in separate containers, and ski training for the men of the Regiment."

Still, Moore found opportunities to explore Japan and learn the culture of its peoples. "In early 1946," he recalled, "My friend, Lieutenant Newlon, won a lottery for the opportunity to buy a new American Chevrolet. He jumped at it. And on many weekends thereafter we explored various places on Hokkaido. We improved our language skills and learned a lot about the Japanese culture, people, and customs. The Emperor told them to be very hospitable to Americans, and they were. I made friends with a lot of the Japanese people and they would invite me into their homes for dinner. Otherwise, in my off-duty time, I did a lot of running, skiing, horseback riding, duck hunting, and along with a Japanese friend I raised German shepherd dogs—police pups imported from Nazi Germany. At night I read."

However, Moore's pioneering spirit occasionally affected his judgment. "An incident occurred in May of 1947," he said, "which tragically impressed upon me the results of BAD JUDGMENT. It was during the 'run-off' time when the deep snows were melting, and rivers were running muddy, fast, and far above normal depths. Four of us lieutenants got hold of a 4-man, 5x8' rubber boat (2 canvas seats), with four paddles and launched it into the Toyohira River while in full flood down towards Sapporo. Almost immediately we realized:

1. We'd made a bad mistake in judgment, and

2. We had no life jackets, a critical error in preparation.

The boat was hurled from cliff to cliff by the fast-moving, trash-filled waves. For the first 100 yards, we were both in and out of control of that boat. Finally, we got the hang of it. From then on it was one hell of an adrenaline-rush until we took out 15 miles downstream. We were lucky at first, and we survived primarily because we were a *team*—coordinating paddling and shifting body weights. Teamwork!"

The next day, however, three of Moore's friends asked to borrow the boat so they could have their own whitewater thrill ride. "We accompanied three other officers and a Red Cross girl and they launched into the river. Within three minutes, the boat overturned. They were all thrown into the raging icy water. In the high, fast-moving waves, we lost sight of them and they and the boat were soon unseen. We searched the banks as best we could until dark; no luck. Three of them including the girl turned up later thoroughly chilled, chastened, and frightened. The fourth, a 2nd Lieutenant, newly commissioned, was still missing. The next day Colonel Wilson [the Regimental Commander] put out an order stopping that activity. I was surprised that he did not call us into his office and take us to the woodshed. Possibly, just possibly, he realized that young paratroop officers all had a risk-taking streak in their make-up and he didn't want to stifle it. BUT no more rubber boat rides on the Tayohira—at least during the spring run-off. The missing officer's body was found two weeks later, washed ashore 10 miles downriver."

More than anything, however, duty in Occupied Japan taught Hal about styles of organizational leadership. "On my bosses: I had three different regimental commanders. Two of them, Colonel George O. Pearson and Lt. Colonel A.H. "Harry" Wilson were very impressive, outstanding leaders who set a great example. They both were experienced paratroop commanders, in combat and in garrison. Calm, taciturn, and charismatic. Both were enthusiastic and aggressive when they deemed it necessary to be so. They gave off the impression that they knew what they were doing and were always in control. I never saw them get excited. They didn't talk much, but they had *presence*. They conveyed competence and confidence. They knew soldiers and soldiering. They were great examples to emulate.

The third of my three regimental commanders was exactly opposite the others. He was overweight, unsure of himself, talked a lot but said little. He put out a lot of unnecessary instructions and poorly conceived orders. He was an example of how not to be.

"I was very fortunate to have General Swing as my first Division Commander—the first top General over me. I have already commented on his appearance. That man had *command presence* in spades. His personality and charisma were intensely forceful. He held himself a bit aloof and apart; always seemed to be thinking. His leadership aura penetrated throughout his several thousand-man command; scattered over Northern Japan. He was a stern disciplinarian, yet always concerned in detail about the welfare of his troops. His leadership style helped me all through my career in the Army."

A General Officer should not and cannot be "one of the boys." The top leader in a large civilian organization should not either. Senior Executives should hold themselves a bit apart and aloof. They should not say much, but when they do, it should be well thought out, make good sense, and be completely clear and understandable.

"The officer under whom I served for the longest period in Japan was Major Mansfield. He was always cool, never raised his voice, very perceptive, took no wooden nickels, and was a natural leader. He told me what he wanted to be done and let me run with the ball. He trusted me and I went an extra '2–3 miles' to make sure I would never let him down, never do a shabby job, or never lose his trust. For example, when he sent me, a lieutenant, out to run the periodic training and proficiency jumps involving hundreds of troopers of all ranks, he made me the final decision maker on whether or not an operation would be called off or delayed because of the wind, weather conditions, or any other reason; even if the activity was in progress, and the troops had risen at 2:00 a.m. and traveled miles in convoy to the loading airfield.

"Major Mansfield taught me so very much. One of the most important leadership principles I learned from him was: 'Push the Power Down.' He was dead honest, very candid, and totally self-confident. He wanted straight talk, no waffling. All told, he was a great role model for a young lieutenant, still wet behind the ears."

"In between all these activities, Major Mansfield was my mentor. I didn't know it at the time, and I had never heard of 'mentoring.' Most likely he had not either. But that's what it amounted to. He coached me; he taught me. He passed on his leadership principles, his planning and operations standards, his convictions, and his experiences in problem-solving."

<u>**Moore's Observations, Lessons Learned or Relearned:**</u>

- **Be calm, cool, self-collected, and take no wooden nickels.**
- **Tell your subordinate leaders your standards at the outset and what you expect.**
- **Push the *authority* down to make decisions, but keep**

responsibility for the results. Do not blame subordinates for bad results. Blame yourself for not training them properly or giving poor instructions.

- As you push power and decision-making authority down, you must also push subsequent praise and recognition for outstanding unit performance down as well. *Don't hog the glory for yourself if you want to build a superb team.*

- Be dead honest with those above and below. Totally candid but not harsh. Straight talk.

- Respect your people. Be loyal to them. Loyalty goes up AND down the chain of command.

- •Taking care of your people is not just about the obvious things—pay, working conditions, concern for their welfare and that of their families—but seeing to it they are properly trained and have the personal discipline and desire to get the job done and done well.

- Treat every person "fair-and-square." No favorites. If you discover subordinates who are uniquely talented, give them the tough jobs and mentor them. It's your duty to help them develop their skills and to learn.

- Keep your people informed. Tell them what's going on: what's coming up, what's hot and what's not.

- Do a lot of listening, especially around the boss. That way you will know at least twice as much—what the speaker knows and what you know. Early on and I can't explain why, on occasion when I was about to say something, a voice inside my head would tell me: "Keep your mouth shut." I always obeyed. I think my instincts were guiding me, and I've always trusted my instincts.

- Carry a notebook or 3x5 cards and take notes when being given instructions or when your boss is explaining his philosophy or guidance on a matter. I also found that when running or doing other physical exercise, ideas and useful thoughts would pop into my head—possibly related in some medical way with blood movement in the brain. So, I took to scrawling notes when running.

- Stay away from higher headquarters or corporate headquarters

unless summoned. No good can come of wandering aimlessly around corridors filled with bosses alert for any sign that someone is underemployed.

After two and a half years in Occupied Japan, Moore received orders to report to the 82nd Airborne Division at Fort Bragg, North Carolina. Departing Camp Crawford, Hal reported to E Company, 1-505th Parachute Infantry Regiment in June 1948. Once again, he found himself a platoon leader but, as was common throughout the postwar Army, there was very little training being done. "Most of what we did was escort the remains of dead American soldiers. There were a lot of World War II dead who had been temporarily buried in Europe and who were being shipped home for burial close to their families." The bodies arrived stateside in a casket which, in turn, was placed inside a cargo crate. A forklift would load the container into the baggage car of a train and Moore would have to stay awake all night in the baggage car, sitting on the floor beside the body. Moore's assignment was to deliver the remains to local morticians across the Southeast—Florida, Georgia, Alabama, and the Carolinas.

After a few months of escort detail, Moore heard about a unit in Fort Bragg "that tested parachutes out of different kinds of airplanes." The Army Field Forces Board had set up a detachment known as the Airborne Test Section, whose sole purpose was to test experimental parachutes for the Army, Air Force, and CIA. Commanded by then-Lieutenant Colonel Harry W.O. Kinnard (Moore's future Division Commander in Vietnam), the unit was seeking volunteers to test the emerging concept of free-fall parachuting, "not the traditional static line methods," which had been used in World War II.

To this point, recreational skydiving was "just gaining traction" in Europe—and the US Army wanted to test its military application for higher altitude air insertions. The Air Force, meanwhile, wanted to test the concepts for pilot ejections. The job sounded exciting and certainly more upbeat than looking after a dead soldier's casket in a baggage car. Hal volunteered for the program and made his first jump with the Test Section on November 17, 1948.

Testing parachutes, as Moore discovered, certainly was exciting—he nearly lost his life on the first jump. That afternoon, as Moore exited the aircraft, his parachute got caught on the plane's tail fin. Suddenly, Moore found himself being dragged through the air at over 120 miles per hour—with both pilots unaware a jumper had been caught on the tail of their aircraft. Luckily, "the parachute tore free, and I was able to activate my reserve."

If you're suddenly hit with an event which could kill you or destroy your business, stay calm and think your way out of it. Don't panic. You *can* handle an immediate, time-critical, sure-death situation and survive. Stay calm and quickly determine what to do and *do it*.

"I served in that duty for nearly 33 months. I jump-tested, experimental canopy releases; equipment bags carrying up to 106 pounds; parachute harnesses, parachutist life preservers (into Tampa Bay and Pamlico Sound), the experimental T-9 and T-10 parachutes, free-fall parachutes, along with miscellaneous signal items, weapons, and helmets. I had several more malfunctions, but I only had to use my reserve chute one other time. On July 26, 1949, I was test jumping the experimental XB-14 Free Fall (no static line opener) Air Force parachute designed for fighter-bomber pilots. It was my ninth jump with that chute; I had to pull a ripcord to activate it. When I pulled the ripcord, the18-inch diameter pilot chute pulled out only a few feet of the suspension lines. Eight feet of lines and the entire canopy remained hung up and stowed in the deployment bag. *It was a complete malfunction.* When I looked up, I saw the pilot chute circling around over my head and realized if I pulled my reserve at the wrong time, it would tangle with the pilot chute, and I would be killed. I had to pull my reserve at the exact instant the pilot chute was beginning to circle around my right shoulder to my rear. I did one mental rehearsal and pulled. I was already dropping at terminal velocity—176 feet per second. My reserve opened with such a shock that the XB-14 broke loose and it opened as well. This was about five to ten seconds before impact. I drifted in slowly under both chutes." With the two parachutes deployed, Moore swayed back and forth like a pendulum through the air as he floated to the ground. After that, Lieutenant Colonel Kinnard gave Moore the nickname "Lucky"—a name that stuck for the remainder of their professional relationship. Aside from these hair-raising tales, however, most of Moore's jumps passed without incident. "I never got seriously injured," he said, "a sprained ankle here and there." His time in the Airborne Section nonetheless reinforced his perspectives on leadership:

Don't let setbacks derail you from continuing your path.

In any profession or organization, there are bound to be hiccups. There may even be catastrophes or close-calls with disaster. Don't let these events break your stride or derail you psychologically from achieving what you want to achieve. At times, life will hit you hard and teach you lessons you have no desire to learn. When the "hits" and setbacks come, a leader simply picks himself up and keeps moving forward.

While honing his skills as a test parachutist, Moore also courted the young Julia B. Compton. Born on February 10, 1929 at Fort Sill, Oklahoma, "Julie," as she was called, was the only child of Colonel and Mrs. Louis J. Compton. She was attending the University of North Carolina—Chapel Hill when she met the young Lieutenant Moore in August 1948. "That summer," Moore said, "while at the Officer's Club swimming pool, she walked over and said, 'Hi, I'm Julie Compton.' That was it!" Captivated by the nineteen-year-old beauty, Moore recalled that "I burned up the roads between Fort Bragg and Chapel Hill during the next year and a half, courting the woman I knew was meant for me." Moore proposed in the spring of 1949, and the couple set their marriage date for November 22 of that year.

As a humorous aside, Colonel Compton, a devoted artillery officer commissioned in 1917 during the "brown shoe," intensely traditional Army of World War I, was mortified his daughter wanted to marry an infantryman. The infantry and artillery branches have a long-standing rivalry within the US Army. After putting in an appearance at the engagement party, Colonel Compton protested the union by retiring to the basement with a fellow artillery colonel whose daughter had also made the mistake of loving an infantryman. While the guests were upstairs enjoying the party, the heretofore tee-totaling Colonel Compton drank away his sorrows with a bottle of bourbon…while polishing the barrel of a brass cannon he had brought home from Germany after World War II. Shortly after that, Compton took a strong liking to Hal and accepted him as a full member of the family.

"Julie would prove to be one of the most respected Army wives ever known." She would later be remembered for "raising holy hell" with commanders and officials in Washington for the way they handled death notifications to next-of-kin during the opening days of the Vietnam War. "She grew up in a military family," Moore recalled, "as Colonel Compton led his family in service to America. Julie understood what serving America meant from a military family perspective. She knew the pains, the sacrifices, the loneliness, the responsibilities, and the joys. I fell in love with a 'leader of the highest kind.' Never for one minute did I forget or take for granted who I married and the five children we were blessed with."

But as Hal and Julie began their lives as a married couple, a war was brewing on the Korean Peninsula.

SUMMARY:

Even in the midst of defeat, carry yourself professionally and maintain your discipline. That is the quickest way towards recovery.

A good leader studies the culture of wherever he is planning to go—and he ensures his subordinates are properly educated on the same.

When in charge, take charge; but treat your subordinates with respect, dignity, and common courtesy.

A worker's performance often reflects the attitude of his leadership.

In the civilian world, the NCOs are the intermediate supervisors. The leader at the top should consult with and visit them frequently, on their turf, to learn more about what goes on down where the job gets done. It will help him make better decisions in future planning, and in assuring better performance. In the Army, the saying is: "An outfit does well the things the boss checks up on."

Wherever possible, solve problems at the lowest level.

Praise in public, Punish in private.

At an official reception, or dinner party, the real purpose of the event is to socialize, to talk with the other guests and participants—eating and drinking is secondary.

A General Officer should not and cannot be "one of the boys." The top leader in a large civilian organization should not either. Senior executives should hold themselves a bit apart and aloof. They should not say much, but when they do, it should be well thought out, make good sense, and should completely clear and understandable.

If you're suddenly hit with an event which could kill you, stay calm and think your way out of it. Don't panic. You can handle an immediate, time-critical, sure-death situation, and survive. Stay calm and quickly determine what to do and do it.

Don't let setbacks derail you from continuing your path.

TRIAL BY FIRE

Korea had been a Japanese colony from its annexation in 1910 until the end of World War II. Following the Allied victory, the United States and the Soviet Union divided the peninsula into two political zones along the 38th Parallel. The North became a Communist state while the south remained Capitalist. However, on June 25, 1950, the North Korean People's Army (NKPA) stormed across the 38th Parallel with the goal of reuniting the peninsula under Communist rule.

"By June 1951, a year after it began," Moore recalled, "the war had generally stalemated across the line where it began—the 38th parallel. It was clear that Russia, America, and Red China wanted peace. Peace talks began in July 1951, but there was no agreement on a Cease-Fire. Meanwhile, the Chinese and North Koreans established defenses in depth for miles – heavily dug-in bunkers covered with tree trunks and earth; deep trenches, underground tunnels, caves, and large rooms. United Nations forces did the same but not anywhere near the extent of the enemy. It was like World War I trench warfare, recon patrols, ambush patrols and brutally savage outpost battles."

"By this time, the great offensives had ended. But for over two years— until the Armistice in August 1953—meat grinder, desperate, local battles continued. These resulted in more casualties on both sides than during the entire first year of the war. In America, Korea became 'The Forgotten War' except to the relatives of those who were involved in it. But to the men who fought in the ferocious hilltop and outpost battles at Punch Bowl, Heartbreak Ridge, Bloody Ridge, Bloody Angle, Yonchon, Old Baldy, Triangle Hill, T-Bone, White Horse Mountain, Sniper Ridge, and

Pork Chop Hill, it was a *very* real war indeed."

"These volcanic blood baths would suddenly boil up across a small strip of the front, on one of our outposts, or on one of the enemy hills, as one side or the other would attack for one reason or another such as, in the final days, to affect the future location of portions of the Demilitarized Zone (DMZ). For miles on either side of the smoking slaughter and destruction there could be no action whatsoever. After the blood bath, it was back to patrolling."

Moore arrived in Korea as a young captain in July 1952 and left in August 1953. "During those 13 months," he said, "I commanded a Rifle Company and a Heavy Mortar Company on the line with the 17th Infantry Regiment, was the Regimental Operations Officer, and ended up as the Assistant 7th Infantry Division Plans and Operations Officer. I spent five months in that last duty under four different Plans and Operations Officers and two different Division Commanders. *I* was the continuity and stability in that job—and on occasion, the top guy. Before being ordered back to Division Headquarters, I'd served under three different 17th Regimental Commanders."

Less than a week after arriving in Korea, Moore took command of the Regiment's heavy mortar company. At first, the prospect of taking over a new company in a combat zone—while trying to learn the culture of the Regiment—seemed overwhelming. However, in a letter written to Julie on July 6, 1952, he reported "by now, I have my feet a bit more firm on the ground—it will take about three more weeks, however, until I really get to know all the various SOPs [Standard Operating Procedures], officers, etc. in the Regiment."

Hal looked forward to leading his new troops, but was not impressed with the company's departing commander. "The fellow who has this company leaves on the 8th [of July]," he wrote. "He will turn the company over to me tomorrow. From what I've seen so far, this is a pretty good bunch of men, but plenty needs shaping up. The present company commander is an obscene, loud, rabbit-faced person who is interested only in getting back to the USA. The Colonel had him pegged, though, as he told me that he [the departing commander] had lost interest in the company. Apparently, all that he is interested in is cheating on his wife as he is continually boasting of his affairs in the past, and to come, en route to his home, wife, and children. I can tell he has no character whatsoever and I can hardly wait for him to leave so I can shake this company up. There'll be some changes made."

In fact, Moore relished the opportunity. He maintained that:

**If given a choice between taking over a good outfit or
a bad outfit, I'll choose the bad outfit every time.
They'll have nowhere to go but up.**

Indeed, after a few days with the company, Moore realized what a
great group of men he had. It was a shame their previous commander
had been such a toxic leader. "The men have been abused," he wrote. The
NCOs had been shunned, the subordinate officers had been alienated,
and they were frequently under-fed—"so I have my work cut out for
me." Moore immediately made it known that a new command climate
was in effect. He broke down the barriers of distrust among his officers
and NCOs by seeking their advice on tactical matters, and his men
reciprocated by educating their commander on the intricacies of mortar
and fire support. Thus it showed:

**There are two things a leader can do: he can either
contaminate his environment with his attitudes and actions, or
he can inspire confidence.**

"One of my first acts as CO [commanding officer] was to move six
men out of the worst 'boar's nest' in the place." These six mortarmen had
been billeted in a derelict bunker which was infested with rodents. "I
moved them into the officer's bunkers and I moved us down there [into the
mortermen's old bunker]. I had some Korean support troops clean it first,
though, and it is very adequate for my Gunnery Officer, Recon Officer,
Warrant Officer, and myself. A few mice and bugs, but not bad. One corner
of my end was dug into an old Korean grave which was immediately
covered, but there is a lingering odor. I keep my feet down at that end, and
by liberal use of an aerosol bomb and opening the door, it's not bad sleeping
at all. These graves are hard to avoid since they are scattered helter-skelter
all over these hills where our positions are." He also took the initiative to
build showers for the platoons and the company command post. "It beats
an hour round trip on the dusty roads to the Regimental shower point,"
Hal said. "The men are cleaner – and whether they realize it or not, they
are near their place of duty and available for fire missions."

These simple acts of compassion strengthened Hal Moore's power
base tenfold. Once his men realized he cared for them and their welfare,
the company's morale (and performance) skyrocketed. Indeed, his initial
actions as Company Commander underscored the fundamental truths of
leadership in an austere environment:

- Good leaders don't wait for official permission to try out a new idea. In any organization, if you go looking for permission, you will inevitably find the one person who thinks his job is to say "No!" It's easier to get forgiveness than permission.

- Put the welfare of your troops above your own. They eat before you eat; they sleep before you sleep.

- Simple acts of courtesy and graciousness have a profound impact on a subordinate's morale, self-perception, and performance. This is particularly the case if a leader takes over an organization that has previously suffered from toxic leadership. Conversely, toxic behavior will destroy morale and lead to subordinates seeing themselves as subpar or defective.

- Subordinates want to feel that the leader "has their back" and is looking out for them. They cannot perform well for a leader who treats them as an inconvenience or who targets them with spiteful vendettas.

- Commanders are not always leaders. Commanders are appointed. Leaders are unofficially "elected" by the troops in the unit. Likewise in other fields of endeavor. Every leader is put through an informal process in the first few weeks wherein his people judge him and decide whether or not he is worthy of their trust. He must earn that trust. How? A leader must prove himself by his actions, appearance, demeanor, attitude, and decisions.

- Most importantly, a leader proves himself by demonstrating his concern for and relationship with the people under him. The old adage: "Take care of your people and they will take care of you."

One month into his command, Hal Moore was the busiest he had ever been. As part of the company's leadership change, he had been given two new NCOs—both of whom had combat experience in World War II—and a crop of new lieutenants. "This is a really good job I have," he wrote to Julie. "No boredom of sitting on the Main Line of Resistance looking through a hole in the bunker." Instead, he spent considerable time moving along the Regimental front coordinating mortar fire among the battalions.

To this point, Moore had noticed that the Regiment's actions had been limited to taking prisoners and conducting small-scale raids. Yet, per Regimental orders, his mortarmen had to stay behind the Main Line of Resistance. This was problematic because the Heavy Mortar Company could not provide close fire support to the frontline patrols from that far away. Thus, Hal Moore took the initiative to reorganize the fire support scheme and coordinate his efforts with local commanders. These actions reinforced one of his primary leadership principles:

A leader must ask himself two things:
What I am doing that I should not be doing?
And what am I *not* doing that I should be doing?

He quickly realized that he should not be complacent with the tactical status quo. Likewise, he discovered he should be thinking of and seeking ways to improve the delivery of mortar fire in support of the Regiment's mission. The same attitude holds true in the business world—the companies that thrive (and survive) are the ones who adapt to changes in the marketplace and continually analyze how to improve the delivery of their products and services. This is not to say that a leader should seek change simply for the sake of change or try to find deficiencies where none exist. As the old saying goes: "If it isn't broken, don't fix it." If a system is already yielding good results, don't feel compelled to change it unless your idea will qualitatively improve the organization's performance. If your good idea backfires, however, don't be too proud to admit your mistake and return things to the way they were previously. Subordinates will respect a leader who admits his errors and says "I was wrong," rather than a leader who makes excuses and looks for something to blame.

In Hal Moore's case, the self-imposed question of what he should or should not be doing produced incredible results. By coordinating with the adjacent Regiments, Moore would move a patrol to the Outpost Line of Resistance every night. He would discuss the fire support plan with the patrol leaders the day before the mission and let them make adjustments based on where they felt they needed the heaviest mortar concentration. If a patrol got lost, Moore would fire White Phosphorous rounds against certain landmarks so the patrol could trace its way back to friendly lines. "I have walked patrols back which couldn't possibly have executed a proper withdrawal because of carrying wounded and equipment. On three separate mornings recently, both Battalion Commanders on the line and the Regimental Commander have complimented the mortar company at the morning briefing."

Apparently, the Regimental Commander liked Moore's handling of the mortarmen so much that he appointed him to be the Regimental Operations Officer (S-3). A billet typically occupied by a Major, the S-3 was responsible for planning maneuvers and training operations. It was an awesome responsibility for a young Captain, but Moore remained confident he could handle the job. "The only thing is, I must become familiar with about thirty different offensive, defensive, and counterattack plans in addition to handling the current operation."

On his last night with the mortar company, Hal recalled a vicious firefight between an American patrol and an enemy ambush. "I had a platoon well forward of the Outpost Line of Resistance to support a long-range patrol. The patrol ran into a Chinese ambush, was surrounded, and had quite a fight. Those four tubes fired all night from 2130 [9:30 p.m.] to 0945 using 845 High Explosive and 755 White Phosphorous. It prevented the Chinese from reinforcing, and covered the patrol's withdrawal. The mortar position took 79 incoming rounds—one right through the FDC [Fire Direction Center] bunker—no one wounded and nothing went out of action. I was awful proud of these men as I know they had a lot to do with preventing that patrol from really being cut up. So I left the company with a good action."

On leading troops in combat, Moore commented that the leader "must be visible on the battlefield; he must be in the battle, battalion commander on down—brigade and division commander on occasion. *He must exhibit his determination to prevail no matter what the odds or how desperate the situation.* He must have and display the will to win by his actions, his words, the tone of his voice on the radio and face-to-face, his appearance, his demeanor, his countenance, the look in his eyes. He must remain calm and cool—no fear. He must ignore the dust, the noise, the smoke, the explosions, the screams of the wounded, the yells, or the dead lying around him—that is all normal. He must never give off any hint or evidence that he is uncertain about a positive outcome, even in the most desperate situations." Crisis management is not unique to the military and civilian leaders must show these same characteristics in stressful situations.

Within a few weeks of becoming the Regimental S-3, Moore had drafted the plans for three anti-airborne operations, three minor penetration plans, three Regimental attacks, and made a complete reconnaissance of the 7th Division's sector. Taken together, these tasks gave Hal Moore a recurring 17-hour workday. Occasionally, he would work for as long as 60 hours without sleep. "To be effective at all this," he said, "I had to know the personalities of the subordinate commanders and their units' combat effectiveness. I also had to study in detail by ground reconnoiter (on foot and by jeep) the territory, terrain, and geography of the area of operations for which we were responsible. I took every opportunity to walk the frontlines to visit and study all positions; every outpost and the surrounding ground, to look at enemy attack routes and friendly counter-attack routes, and know the locations of all roads to, from, and across the front."

For Hal Moore, being the Regimental Operations Officer also reinforced the importance of *mentoring*. "The Regimental Executive Officer, Lt. Colonel Ted Mataxis, took a liking to me," said Moore. "He had served as an Infantry battalion commander in the European Theater during World War II, and as a United Nations Observer when India and Pakistan were formed as independent countries in the late 1940s. He would frequently talk with me late at night instructing me, giving me the benefit of his experiences and guidance." As Moore recalled, these mentoring sessions were helpful because: "A leader must realize his subordinate leaders will be killed or wounded. He must prepare and train other leaders to step up and take over. He, himself, must train his next-in-line to take command in the event he is killed, wounded, or evacuated."

Moore's Observations, Lessons Learned or Re-learned:

- **I'd been taught for years that leaders must *set the example* and tried to do so. But in battle, it is absolutely mandatory—and especially so during the Korean War at the company level.**

- **I learned that I could keep calm and functional in the bedlam, stress, noise, blood, and killings of a fierce battle. I had no choice but to remain calm.**

- **Stay in shape. When we were not in a battle or other operation, I took a run in the late afternoon for an hour or so.**

- **The first reports from the battlefield are usually exaggerated for good or bad, and are not entirely accurate. This is normal, since they are sent back by leaders in a moving battle and are fragmentary.**

- **Operations journals must be meticulously kept. Entries must be accurate as reported. An entry, once made, can never be changed.**

- **When the Colonel (or later, the General) grew to trust me** that I did my homework and had my act together, they would usually accept my recommendations. As a staff officer I had a desk at Headquarters and worked from about 7:00 a.m. until late at night. I never wanted to lose the trust the Colonel or the General had placed in me.

Moore's next combat actions occurred later that fall. In September 1952, General James Van Fleet, the Eighth US Army Commander, submitted plans for Operation Showdown, a low-level attack designed to push the Chinese defensive line 1,250 yards farther north. The decisive point of the attack focused on a ridgeline two kilometers wide near Kimwha. Dominated by three hills, the forested ridge was known as the Triangle Hill Complex. The following month, as peace negotiations stalled at Panmunjom, the Chinese launched preparatory strikes along the 7th Division's Main Line of Resistance.

Moore was both amazed and disgusted by the enemy's tactics. Throughout the battle, the Chinese sent waves of infantrymen through their own artillery screen. This led to mass incidents of fratricide. The few Chinamen who made it through the artillery screen, however, did so with such unflinching precision that Moore thought they must have been under the influence of drugs. "They take a lot of casualties," he marveled, "but don't seem to care."

By the end of October, however, most of the action had died down. Throughout the engagement, Chinese forces had sustained more than 4,000 casualties. This catastrophic loss of manpower left them with only one division to fight the UN forces on Triangle Hill. But the Chinese refused to quit. "We had our 2nd and 3rd Battalions on Triangle Hill," Moore said, "and a Chinese Regiment counterattacked." During the engagement, the 3rd Battalion had every officer in all three of its rifle companies wounded or killed, and each company was cut down to less than 100 men before being relieved by a battalion from the 32nd Regiment.

"Just before the 7th Division attack on Triangle Hill," he recalled, "one of the battalion commanders whose unit was to attack told me he was very apprehensive about accomplishing his mission. I thought to myself that with his attitude, he would not be successful and would get a lot of his men killed. As it turned out, I was right. He was relieved of his command." Moore's biggest takeaway from the encounter was:

Before going into battle (or while you're in a battle), or undertaking a tough project or competition, if you, the leader, think you might lose, then you have already lost.

By October 25, General Van Fleet pulled the 7th Division off Triangle Hill and turned the area over to the South Korean (ROK) 2nd Division. The battle continued for another month but, in the face of mounting UN casualties, Van Fleet halted the ROK's attack on November 28. Shortly thereafter, Chinese forces re-occupied the hill. Triangle Hill would go down in history as the bloodiest battle of 1952. For Hal Moore, though, the battle had been an exercise in futility. UN Forces had occupied the land surrounding Triangle Hill, then quit the field and let the Communists reoccupy the area. He left the battle with a firm conviction that a leader should:

Never give up ground. It will cost more casualties to take it back than holding on to it in the first place.

Following the Triangle Hill action, the Division moved the Regiment off the line to spend a month guarding hardcore Chinese prisoners near Koje-Do. Moore described them and the new assignment in late November, "This is quite unique duty down here. Very interesting. Every now and then, these birds act up. I have my own private belief that this PW Camp is a powder keg." By the end of December, the situation worsened, "Higher headquarters is quite concerned that these PW are going to attempt an outbreak. I know that if they do start something, it will be quite a bloody mess. It has to be nipped in the bud fast if it does. 48,000 PW could really stampede once started." After a few small riots, Moore took action to prevent escalation. He realized that the long Chinese logistics trail emphasized critical supplies for combat operations, ammunition and food, not comfort items. While in the PW camps, the Chinese prisoners could enjoy the creature comforts the American logistics system included as a matter of course; notably, toilet paper.

Following a riot, Moore removed all the toilet paper from the camps and put the word out it would not be returned until behavior improved. Within one biological cycle, things settled down and, other than some minor infractions, the prisoners gave the 17th Regiment no further problems. Moore had identified the situational "center of gravity" of the enemy. Think of this example when confronted with a competitive challenge. Ask yourself, "What's the toilet paper?" Crude, but easy to understand. In mid-January, the unit moved back to the front.

Shortly after the 7th Division occupied its new sector near T-Bone Hill, Moore learned that he had been recommended for an early promotion to Major. Apparently, his performance as the S-3 had inspired the Regimental Commander to make the recommendation. Before Hal could pin on his new rank, however, an unexpected twist of fate put him in command of a rifle company. Per the 7th Division's policy, an Infantry captain could not be promoted to major until he had commanded a rifle platoon or company in combat. Moore had commanded a rifle platoon, but it had been with the Army of Occupation in Hokkaido – and according to the General's policy, Moore's previous command of the mortar company held no weight. Thus, Hal could not be promoted until he had commanded a rifle company on the frontline.

Hal Moore assumed command of K Company (3rd Battalion, 17th Infantry) on February 4, 1953. Just as he had done with the mortar company, Hal realized that he had inherited a unit which suffered from poor leadership. The previous commander, he noticed, was remarkably similar to the one he had replaced in the mortar company. "This company is sadly lacking in discipline…the men are unnecessarily dirty," he wrote. "I am in the process of shaping up a few platoon leaders, including two 2nd Lieutenants of the [West Point] Class of '51." Even though he had inherited another jaded company, Moore relished the opportunity. Writing home to Julie, he brimmed that: "With the right motivation and leadership, they have nowhere to go but up."

K Company covered nearly half of the battalion's Main Line of Resistance. To accommodate this vast defensive area, the battalion augmented Moore's company with a platoon from nearby L Company, a tank platoon, and a section of anti-aircraft guns. "I am defending a critical sector," he wrote, "and I think we're fairly well disposed. I am making a few changes, though. The company itself is falling out hard and I am cracking the whip on my platoon leaders. I love command duty anyway and nothing pleases me more than to shape up a unit."

Moore also realized that K Company's previous commander had created a culture of divisiveness within the unit. There seemed to be an "us versus them" mentality between the combat soldiers and the support soldiers assigned to the formation. Thus, in the spirit of inclusiveness (and ensuring that every soldier maintained his basic fighting skills), Moore wrote "I have cooks, drivers, typists—'clerks and jerks'—all formed up as a local reserve as all my platoons are on line. I keep a loaded grease gun [M-3 submachine gun] hanging right on my rack along with three magazines of ammo. I can be out of here and moving within five minutes if any of my people get hit."

Be ready, so you don't have to *get* ready. A good leader will

pre-position as many assets and people as he can before an event, or as a contingency in case of disaster. Thus, when the alert and/or emergency inevitably comes, you will be better prepared to respond to it.

Reflecting on his time at the battlefront, Moore recalled that Korea was oddly reminiscent of World War I. "In Korea," he said, "we had deep communications trenches. We called them 'commo' trenches— six to eight feet deep. Some had duckboards on the bottom; most did not. When it rained or snowed, it was a deep muddy mess. There were offshoot trenches leading to fire steps and fighting positions on the spine and slopes of the hills. Also, off the main trench, were dug-outs used as command posts and for ammo storage. The surrounding terrain, devoid of any growth, was typical of all positions. The surface of the earth for hundreds of yards around had long since been changed into a moonscape of pits and holes from the artillery shell and bomb explosions.

"There was a very foul stink on these positions…the combined odors of lime-sprinkled latrines, sour-smelling dirty clothes and dirty men, wet earth and sandbags, mud, stale coffee, cleaning oil, and gunpowder. Under a hot sun, this unique perfume was thick enough to cut. Occasionally, in digging trench extensions or new firing positions, long-dead human remains were uncovered which added to the smell. The daily program for the men was the maintenance of trenches, bunkers, barbed wire, firing positions, weapons, and preparation of new entrenchments. When the monsoon torrents came in July and August, our clothes, trenches, and boots were filthy, muddy and wet for weeks."

"The Chinese positions were very tough to crack. They were hard-core, heavy-duty, professional diggers. Their lines were deeply entrenched, with extensive cave systems, catacombs, and large underground rooms. Our artillery, bombers, and close air support had little to no effect against these. The Chinese would dig a cave straight back into a ridge or a hillside and place a long-range artillery piece in it. They'd roll it out, fire ten to twenty rounds at us, and then wheel it back in. By the time our counter-fire batteries could fix the location, and our artillery could shoot back at the mouth of the cave, the enemy gun was safe, and its crew back inside sucking down their rice." Years later, Moore noted that the Viet Minh used the same tactics against the French at Dien Bien Phu—"surely on the prompting of their Chinese advisers."

During these outpost battles in Korea, Moore also noted that "the Chinese did not use envelopments or flank attacks," like many had expected they would. "Mostly night attacks," he said, "in waves, straight at the hill." During these attacks, "they used bugles, whistles, flares, flashlights, runners, shouting, and hand and arm signals for control. No radios. Once a fight began, it quickly came down to intense mortar and artillery fire from both sides." These artillery duels were often punctuated by three to five-man skirmishes, close-in trench warfare.

"On the line, we tried to feed our men three hot meals a day. This meant rotating the troops in the trenches off the line behind the hill to a chow bunker where they would eat food ladled into their mess kits by the cooks. Most days we could feed our men three hot meals. The other meal was a C-ration [canned, pre-cooked meals]. During a fierce battle like Pork Chop Hill it was all C-rations. Men don't eat much in combat but need a lot of water. *And I mean a lot.* Smoke, dust, heat, tension, used-up energy…fighting is hard work.

"We manned all trenches day and night. About every twenty yards, there was a firing step or slot. In the daytime, we tried to get every man a few hours of sleep in a sleeping bunker, alternating units. These bunkers had several narrow racks [beds] made out of commo [radio] wire. In the firing positions, we usually had two racks."

"My CP was typical: dug deep into the back of the top of a hill. Heavy timbers, earth floor, and a roof covered with sandbags. I had an M-1943 Yukon Diesel oil stove on the ground in the bunker, and always a can on the stove with hot coffee in it. My artillery forward observer, our radio operators, and I slept when we could in our GI mummy sleeping bags on those WD-30 commo wire racks. We slept with our boots and clothes on."

"Our serious casualties were evacuated from the battle area almost always in their ponchos. Few litters were available. The WIA were treated by medics (if available) on the spot. If possible, other men would transport them. I have helped carry many WIA and KIA in two wars and I can tell you that a soldier in uniform with weapon, ammo, and gear is a very heavy 4-man load."

"On Pork Chop Hill, the trenches were deep, some covered with timbers. On such positions, when the Chinese got into the system, it was 'bloody difficult,' as the British would say, to find and kill them. They were like a herd of cockroaches in most of the trenches and in a lot of the bunkers. Friendlies—dead and alive—were mixed in with the enemy and reduced to doing battle singly or in groups of two to five men at the most. All actions were separated from one another. Except for the tell-tale sound of small arms or languages being spoken, it was impossible to identify friendly from the enemy in the shadows, smoke, and dust."

After less than a month in command, Moore was recalled to Division Headquarters to be appointed the Assistant Division Operations Officer (G-3), concurrent with his promotion to Major. "I guess he [General Smith] considers me purified with a rifle company now," Moore later wrote. "During my time with K Company, I lost more men from enemy shelling than the entire battalion did in six weeks of patrol actions. The principal reason was that I defended a critical flank and had some tanks and AAA [anti-aircraft artillery] on my Main Line of Resistance. As a result, we were the recipients of Chinese harassing, interdictory, and destruction fire all day long—varying in intensity from day to day."

Reflecting on his command of K Company, Moore offered the following lessons:

- **When everything's quiet on the line and nothing's going wrong, tighten up the security and be sure the listening posts and outposts are alert; especially at night and particularly if it's raining or snowing. That's the most opportune time for the enemy to close in.**

- **Be sure that deserving men are decorated with the appropriate awards for valor or meritorious action. Fewer things will impact a team's morale than a leader who does not recognize their accomplishments and hard work.**

- **When reporting information to higher headquarters during battle, send back the reports exactly as received. Do not embellish or diminish.**

- **VERY IMPORTANT: When you draw up a plan of attack or defense, you must have information on weather, terrain, and enemy capabilities but you cannot coordinate your plan with the enemy. Therefore, think through all the "what if's"—what if the enemy does this; what if this or that happens. It's time well spent.**

- **Soldiers in battle fight, kill, and die primarily for each other.**

Moore's new position as Assistant G-3 gave him a bird's eye view of all the regiments stationed along the 7th Division front. Within a month of his arrival, he was making regular trips to the frontline to assess the situation on the ground and relay reports to Division Headquarters. During one of these trips, however, the Chinese suddenly renewed their offensive. This time, the action focused on Hill 266—the dominant terrain feature in a craggy area known as "Old Baldy." Twelve miles northeast of Panmunjom, Old Baldy had been the site of four previous battles. Each time, the Communists had failed to take the hill. Now, in March 1953, the Chinese were making their final bid for Hill 266.

From March 23-26, 1953, Moore was caught on the frontline as the Chinese directed their assault on Old Baldy. The trip nearly cost him his life. During a firefight one morning, Moore and another soldier took cover behind a revetment. As they looked over the top of the barricade to assess the enemy situation, the other soldier promptly took a bullet to the head. Moore cringed as the young soldier fell dead at his feet. "I tried not to think about it. You have to keep your head clear and just let the chips fall where they may." Moore was devastated by the sudden demise of his comrade, but he had to keep his "head in the fight" if he wanted to survive.

"In battle," he said, "it's a 'crapshoot' whether or not you get shot, or hit by shrapnel from an exploding shell, or step on a mine." During that same firefight, Moore recalled that "a Chinese 82 mm mortar shell exploded a few yards away from me *at the exact moment* I looked down to my right. At that instant, my steel helmet was struck and dented deeply over my right eye by a shell fragment." Typically, a mortar would have killed anyone standing that close. The shock wave catapulted Moore head over heels and, when he regained consciousness a few seconds later, he realized that he had been thrown approximately thirty feet. "I was momentarily stunned," he continued, "my helmet still strapped on but sideways. I reached down and picked up a jagged piece of steel that was the size of a crumpled-up cigarette pack and immediately dropped it. *Red hot!* Had I not looked down at the instant of explosion, it would have gone into my head. It's a crapshoot." After the battle, he maintained that only the grace of God had saved him.

A few months after the Battle of Old Baldy, the negotiating parties at Panmunjom finally reached an accord. The armistice—signed on July 27, 1953—restored the international boundary at the 38th Parallel and established the Korean Demilitarized Zone (DMZ). Moore happily returned to the United States, but he left Korea with a firm conviction the US had sabotaged its own success. Although the Americans claimed victory, they had merely fought the Communists to a draw. Moore also noted that the Army's rules of engagement tended to discourage initiative rather than promote it.

"After Korea," he said, "I served three years at West Point, teaching

Infantry tactics to cadets." Coincidentally, one of these cadets was H. Norman Schwarzkopf, who would later command Coalition forces during the Persian Gulf War. Years later, Schwarzkopf cited Moore as one of his personal heroes and credited Moore as the reason he chose to be an Infantry officer. "During the summer," Moore recalled, "we were outdoors on the reservation and the cadets were active in the field, day and night, on military exercises and firing various weapons." During the academic year, however, classes were held indoors—giving lectures to approximately 200 cadets during the two hours immediately following lunch—right when the audience was most drowsy. "Whenever possible," though, "I livened up my classes with skits, film excerpts, and cadet participation. These were the first lectures I had ever given. It was a learning experience that's stood me in good stead ever since."

Moore's Observations, Lessons Learned or Relearned:

- **Rehearse your talk; orally if possible. If not, read it to yourself as if you were speaking. Get the time down.**

- **If possible, check the venue of the talk beforehand to understand lighting, podium/speaker's platform/holder or table for notes, functionality of technical gear (slide projector or equivalent, laser or other type pointer, video system), how the Q&A will be handled, the sound system, outside noise, etc.**

- **The first impression a speaker makes on his audience is by his appearance and demeanor. Well-groomed or not? Self-Confident or not? Nervous or not? Paper-shuffler or not? All this and more before he says a word. The next impression is how the speaker talks. Forceful or not? Correct diction or not? Too much use of hands? Walking around? If so, too much? Any distracting mannerisms (such as always shoving his spectacles back up his nose)? Speaks too loud? Too soft? "Talks down" to the audience? The next impression is about what he says—the content of his talk. Are the thoughts well-organized? Or is he just "winging it?"**

- **Unless the speaker is a stand-up comic and is speaking as such, I'm not impressed with those who start out with a joke or the ones who waste my time telling me how happy he is to be here.**

- **Probably the best lesson I learned is that a speaker must be** carefully prepared.

- **In my duty at West Point, I again took advantage of the magnificent library and stayed in great shape by running and playing singles handball.**

Upon concluding his tour at the Academy, Moore attended the US Army Command and General Staff College (CGSC) at Fort Leavenworth, Kansas for a yearlong course of study. Renowned as one of the toughest schools in the Army, CGSC prepared young Majors for the organizational dynamics of Division and Corps-level staff. Moore then reported to the Air Mobility Division in the Office of the Chief of Research and Development at the Pentagon.

"At Fort Bragg, I jump-tested experimental parachutes and other equipment developed for Army paratroopers from various Air Force and Army aircraft. Now, in the Pentagon my responsibility was to monitor the development of that equipment for the Army and work with the Air Force to make sure that Army requirements for hauling and dropping troops and equipment were met in the development of new Troop Carrier airplanes. I made frequent trips to civilian firms and the Army and Air Force agencies charged with the actual hardware development to check up on progress. During many of those visits, I would jump different equipment from various aircraft. I was the only Army officer in the Pentagon on 'jump pay'—an extra $100 a month.

"Those years, 1957-1960, also saw the development of the Army's concept for Air Assault and Airmobile tactics. My boss [Lieutenant General James A. Gavin] oversaw all that as well. I was a Major by then and served under three successive full colonels with extensive ground combat experience in World War II: Colonels Jack Norton, Phil Seneff, and Bob Williams. All were very sharp, imaginative officers, and held in high regard by the top generals in the Army and obviously destined for higher rank. All three, in fact, advanced to three-star general. Their time was primarily devoted to fighting for funds to develop the family of Army helicopters and to get the Airmobile/Air Assault concept 'off the ground.' They trusted me completely, told me what they wanted from me; gave me guidance, and let me 'run with the ball.' After my trips to the field, I would write up a 'Trip Report' for them and for my project files, which they could read when fitted into their schedule. These men were fast movers, and I had to move fast, think fast, and turn in good work to keep ahead of the power curve. Workweeks were long: 50-60 hours, Monday—Saturday and I took unclassified papers home with me for night work when my wife and children were in bed."

At the Pentagon, he said, "the pressure and stress level were very high due to the volume of work, long hours, and tight deadlines for decisions involving a lot of money and vast numbers of people. To help control that stress and stay in shape for field duty, every day during lunch hour I either went to the Pentagon Athletic Club and got a workout playing handball or, on alternate days, ran the two miles over to the Lincoln Memorial and back. *I'm a firm believer that physical fitness aids mental fitness.* My wife got used to me coming home after a tough day and telling her I was so tired I was going out for a run. It always refreshed me and cleared my mind to deal with the two briefcases of work I brought home with me.

"There was some very helpful mentoring, especially by Colonel Norton, the only one of my three bosses who was an Army Aviator *and* a fellow Master Parachutist. He had made four combat jumps in World War II: Sicily, Italy, France, and Holland. I will never forget a comment he made to me one day when I was expressing my displeasure over an on-going staff action. He gave me a hard look and said: "OK, I hear you. But what are you *personally doing* to help solve this problem?'" For Hal Moore, the exchange highlighted the following lesson:

Don't complain to your boss. He wants solutions; not just problems.

"In the Pentagon," he continued, "the grunt work is done by so-called 'Action Officers' as I was (majors and lieutenant colonels). Their boss is usually a full colonel, called a "Division Chief," and his boss is a one or two-star General. The next boss is a three-star General who works for the four-star Army Chief of Staff.

"The system works like this: an Action Officer is given a paper which outlines a problem for resolution, or an issue on which a decision is required involving money, training, development of a new vehicle or weapon, an operations issue (like sending troops overseas to a crisis), etc. He works up a proposed solution or decision and walks it around the halls to other appropriate Army staff agencies and coordinates it for information, concurrence, or non-concurrence. Then it's moved up the chain. Often, the Action Officer has to 'brief' orally the paper to Generals or the Army Chief of Staff, or even the civilian Secretary of the Army."

"Frequently, an action was 'time-critical' for one reason or another like a budget decision, a reply to a Congressional question, or an immediate operational decision for troop movement (like what occurred when Iraq invaded Kuwait in 1990). The pressure and tension level was very high on those occasions."

Duty in the Pentagon was rigorous and can also be hard on family life. To beat the Washington traffic and to stay ahead of my bosses, I rose very early and often would not get home until after my wife and our three children (all under 9 years) had eaten dinner. I worked until noon on Saturday and brought work home at night. The cost of living in Washington was very high. My wife always handled our money, and she had quite a juggling job in those years. We did try to do 'family outings' as much as possible. Happiness in the home centers around the wife and mother, and my wife Julie was superb.

Washington and Northern Virginia have always been "High Cost of Living Areas." Add that to the pressure and long hours of work in the Pentagon, and you've got a situation where marriage is placed under stress. Each family has its own situation to deal with. For the marriage and family to survive as a unit and have a sound home life, the husband and wife have to face up to the situation and deal with it. The fact that my wife was born into and raised in the Army helped.

Moore's Observations, Lessons Learned or Relearned

- I discovered I could handle that Pentagon type pressure, and in fact, liked it. In a time–critical action, I could go into kind of a "Zone," think more quickly, incisively, calmly, and meet the requirement.

- If you want to learn fast, if you want to "get ahead," and be advanced up the ladder, it helps to work for sharp bosses and good leaders.

- For any young officer thrown into a turbulent, fast-moving world, the upside is that, almost always, you will work for good bosses who themselves are on the way up. You will encounter Colonels and Generals – some of whom will be Senior Generals leading the Army later on. Most of these men may sit on Promotion Boards or Competitive School Selection Boards in later years. If you work hard and do a good job, you will be remembered.

- Colonel and Mrs. Compton gave me the sound advice to stay extremely well groomed along with the money to purchase a new tailored uniform. I found enough money of my own to get a total of three uniforms and excellent uniform shoes. I made it a point every morning to shine the brass insignia on my uniform and shoes. I always wore clean, carefully pressed uniforms and maintained good haircuts.

- A real downside to the Pentagon was that it's a "desk job." But that "minus" was quickly turned into a "plus" by joining the Pentagon Athletic Club. It was fully equipped with a swimming pool, handball courts, weights, steam room, locker, and a snack bar facility. It was built underground, just outside the 8th Corridor at about a 50-yard walk. I kept in great shape, and it helped to keep the pressure down in the Boiler Room activity of day-to-day work.

- I found quickly in the Pentagon that the Colonel and Generals have grave responsibilities. They have a lot of decisions piling up in front of them—most of which involve a lot of taxpayer money, or involve combat readiness, or wartime decisions, or affect the lives of soldiers and their families. If your work and conscientiousness show your boss he can trust you never to put a sloppy solution in front of him, he will most likely always approve of it.

- KNOW YOUR STUFF. I was often required to sit in on meetings with other Action Officers. Early on, I discovered the officer who'd called the meeting had not, on occasion, thought through a logical plan on how to move the meeting through an issue. From then on, if time permitted, when I was called to a meeting, I would prepare several copies of an agenda which were related to the issue but simultaneously constructed to advance my boss's position. *You can control any meeting with a carefully-designed agenda.*

- When you're an action officer in the Pentagon, you are in a "testing out" job, a learning job. It's a great opportunity to enhance your reputation or damage it. In a civilian corporation, it would be the equivalent of a mid-level management position or sitting on a board of directors.

"In early January 1960, I was ordered to the Armed Forces Staff College in Norfolk, Virginia. The students were from all US Military services along with a few foreign officers from Allied countries. It was a six-month course. From there I was ordered to NATO's Northern

Headquarters located just outside the city of Oslo. The Commander was a Lieutenant General in the British Army." By this time, Moore was a Lieutenant Colonel and recalled his duties were "associated with Ground Forces Plans and Operations for the defense of Northern Germany, Denmark, and Norway. Duty was Monday – Friday, 9:00 a.m. – 4:00 p.m. and Wednesday afternoons free. It was a radical change from the hectic pace of the Pentagon, and one that took me sometime to become comfortable with, and make the necessary mental re-arrangements."

Moore noted that the principles of staff work he learned in the Pentagon worked in Oslo as well, "but being a British-run Headquarters," he said, "it was a slower pace and more low-key." During their three years in Oslo, Hal and Julie became fairly fluent in Norwegian and sent their children to Norwegian schools.

Moore's lifelong belief that subordinates can sense uncertainty in leaders which translates into halting, uncertain and half-hearted execution of orders and decisions was not limited to his professional life. When the family moved to Norway, he had the choice of sending his two sons (8 and 9 years old) to the American School or a Norwegian one—and chose a Norwegian Catholic School. Not only would the lessons be delivered in Norwegian to two small children who did not know a word of the language, but just reaching the school was a challenge. The boys had to walk a half mile to the train station, take a train to the middle of Oslo, and then walk another half mile to the school.

His son, Steve, remembers accepting all of this without hesitation. "There was no hand-wringing between Mom and Dad about whether we could do this. Instead, we were shown how to negotiate the train, the route to school through the city and turned loose. Greg and I never had a doubt about our ability to do this because Dad never had any doubt. We did not think anything of this or were scared, just that it was normal and expected. In other words, Dad instilled the confidence in us that we could do this without a problem.

"I do remember my first day at the school with crystal clarity—my first class was French, taught in Norwegian to a kid who could speak neither. Thankfully, the nuns, in their traditional disciplined way, tutored Greg and I over the next several months in Norwegian and we rapidly became fluent. A related story is that towards the end of the first year, Greg was with some of his Norwegian friends when a lost American couple walked up and asked for directions. The Norwegian kids immediately starting yelling, "Gregory, Gregory!" Greg answered their questions and, as the couple walked away, heard them say, "Amazing! That kid speaks flawless English... no accent."

"Another comment along the lines of self-reliance and self-confidence is that Dad pulled Greg and I aggressively into cross-country skiing to develop our physical capabilities along with the mental. Skis were the gift of choice on our first Christmas and, shortly after that, we were on the innumerable cross-country ski trails that wind like ribbons through the dense woods creating the perimeter of Oslo. Greg and I would take the train up into the surrounding mountains and proceed to ski, by ourselves (at eight and nine), through the surrounding wilderness sometimes returning after dark. We didn't think anything of it, and I can't imagine allowing children as young as we were to wander through the woods on their own in today's world. Cross-country skiing in Norway was a big deal and you could compete for distance skiing awards. On every trail, there was a set of rubber stamps to allow the skier to confirm they had gone the proper distance on a scorecard. Dad enrolled us in the program, and Greg and I skied enough in a single winter to earn the Norwegian Ski Association's gold lapel pin for skiing over 500 km. As far as we know, we were the youngest Americans ever to achieve that distinction. The bottom line is that Dad instilled the self-confidence and will to win in us at an early age—just as he did in every unit he commanded."

"We were in Norway from 1960 to 1963," Hal said. "I was then sent to the US Naval War College in Newport, Rhode Island for a year of Advanced Military Schooling." For Moore, living in Norway reinforced the same lesson he had learned in Occupied Japan:

Get to know the local people, study the language and culture, and take the opportunity to see the country and neighboring countries.

Meanwhile, President Kennedy took a fresh look at air-mobility. During Moore's time in the Pentagon, a strong tide of bureaucratic resentment had put the airmobile concept on the backburner. However, in 1962, at the behest of Secretary of Defense Robert McNamara, the Army convened the Tactical Mobility Requirements Board at Fort Bragg. Headed by General Hamilton Howze, the board's mission was to test the viability of integrating helicopters into the Army's tactical formations. After some deliberation, the board recommended creating an airmobile "test" division equipped with 459 helicopters. This new division would include airmobile infantry battalions and an air cavalry squadron to provide aerial reconnaissance and close air support. For the occasion, the

Army reactivated the 11th Airborne Division in February 1963 and re-designated it the 11th Air Assault Division (Test).

Coincidentally, the 11th Air Assault was commanded by Harry WO Kinnard, Moore's former boss from the Airborne Test Section and now a Major General. "I immediately wrote to him asking for command of a battalion." In those days, a division commander could hand-pick his own battalion commanders. After several months, however, Moore heard nothing back from Kinnard and prepared to take on another assignment at the Pentagon. "But in April 1964, the Army Personnel Office in the Pentagon told me that General Kinnard had asked for me to command one of his battalions in the 11th Air Assault Division."

SUMMARY

If given a choice between taking over a good outfit or a bad outfit, I'll choose the bad outfit every time. They'll have nowhere to go but up.

There are two things a leader can do: he can either contaminate his environment with his attitudes and actions, or he can inspire confidence.

A leader must ask himself two things: What am I doing that I should not be doing? And what am I *not* doing that I should be doing?

Before going into battle (or while you're in a battle), or undertaking a tough project or competition, if you, the leader, think you might lose, then you have already lost.

Never give up ground. It will cost more casualties to take it back than holding on to it in the first place.

Be ready, so you don't have to get ready. A good leader will pre-position as many assets and people as he can before an event, or as a contingency in case of disaster. Thus, when the alert and/or emergency inevitably comes, you will be better prepared to respond to it.

Don't complain to your boss. He wants solutions; not just problems.

Get to know the local people, study the language and culture, and take the opportunity to see the country and neighboring countries.

Moore's parents, Harold Sr. and Mary enjoy an elegant dinner at the 400 Club in New York, circa 1939. Moore credited his mother and father with instilling in him a lifelong devotion to the Catholic faith, servant leadership, integrity, mental toughness, and perseverance. *The Harold G. Moore Collection*

An aerial photograph of West Point at mid-century. It was often said: "If God is an American, He lives in the chapel above West Point." *West Point photo*

A young Cadet Hal Moore stands in front of Central Area Barracks, 1942. Moore never lost sight of his goal—to attend West Point. Although it took him two years to secure an appointment, he never quit, and never said "No" to himself as he pursued his dream. *The Harold G. Moore Collection*

Returning to West Point in 2010, Hal Moore stands with cadets and family members outside the toilet whose 40-watt lightbulb allowed him to study until 2:00 AM as he struggled to understand the arcane mysteries of Calculus and Physics. *The Harold G. Moore Collection*

Hal Moore's graduation portrait, 1945. His inscription in the West Point yearbook read: "Untouched by the machinations of the TD [Tactical Department] and the Academic Departments, Hal never wasted a week-end with inactivity. The casual consistency with which he escorted beautiful young ladies remained a continual source of amazement to his classmates, but as often as not Saturday afternoon found Hal heading for the nearest fishing hole with his favorite tackle. He is ever ready to forsake his more serious pursuits for the harmony of the nearest barber shop quartet or for the joy of all-day ski trip." *West Point photo*

Moore stands in front of the 11th Airborne Division's jump school near Tokyo. After five qualifying jumps from a C-47 aircraft, Moore earned his wings and reported to the 187th Glider Infantry Regiment based in Hokkaido. *The Harold G. Moore Collection*

Moore accompanies General Joseph M. Swing (right), commander of the 11th Airborne Division, during an inspection of troops, 1946. Moore cited General Swing as a lasting example of how higher-echelon leadership should behave. *The Harold G. Moore Collection*

On Occupation Duty in Japan, Moore studied the culture and made the effort to get to know the Japanese people to understand how to operate efficiently within the cultural framework. *The Harold G. Moore Collection*

Hal Moore prepares for a winter jump in Hokkaido, January 1948. *The Harold G. Moore Collection*

Lieutenant Hal Moore in his first stateside portrait, 1949. After serving three years in Occupied Japan, Hal returned to the United States with orders to the 82d Airborne Division at Fort Bragg, North Carolina. *The Harold G. Moore Collection*

Hal Moore (lower right) serves as a "saber bearer" at the wedding of his friend, Lieutenant Joe McCarthy, at a church in Hokkaido. Many of Moore's classmates had destination weddings in Occupied Japan. A few even brought home Japanese war brides. *The Harold G. Moore Collection*

Splashing down in Tampa Bay, Florida, 1949. While assigned to the Airborne Test Section, Moore jump-tested a variety of experimental parachutes and parachute life preservers for the Army, Air Force, and CIA. During his time testing parachutes, Moore learned to stay calm and quickly think his way out of sure-death situations. *The Harold G. Moore Collection*

A young Julie Compton. The daughter of an Army colonel, she met the young Lieutenant Moore while she was attending the University of North Carolina – Chapel Hill. The pair quickly fell in love and were married in the fall of 1949. *The Harold G. Moore Collection*

Hal and Julie on their wedding day, November 23, 1949. As an Army daughter, Army wife and Army mother of two sons who followed their father to West Point, she understood the demands of service life. *The Harold G. Moore Collection*

Captain Hal Moore as the Regimental Operations Officer (S-3) for the 17th Infantry Regiment, 7th Infantry Division. Moore arrived in Korea during the summer of 1952. By this time, the major offenses had ended and the war had devolved into a World War I-style conflict—trench battles with both sides making minor advances against the other. *17th Infantry Regiment Association*

Hal Moore matured as a combat leader during the desperate hilltop battles in Korea. His confidential letters home reflected his horror at how casually troops were thrown against objectives of marginal value. Writing after the Triangle Hill bloodbath, "I could write for hours about this useless slaughter on Hill 598 but would not cover it. All I can say is that General Smith has a lot of blood on his head." Moore considered each soldier precious and agonized over every loss. In a letter home from Vietnam he wrote, "My subconscious is bothering me about my men who were killed. I wake at night thinking of them and how bravely and great they fought. I also have some small idea of the terrible heartbreaking experiences you are going through now with their families. It tore me up to help carry my fine NCOs and men out in ponchos and put them on helicopters." *The Harold G. Moore Collection*

Moore relaxes in front of his outpost command bunker, Spring 1953. *The Harold G. Moore Collection*

A Moore family portrait, 1956. The children seated from left to right are Gregory, Julie, and Steven. As the family settled into postwar life, Hal Moore took on a variety of mid-career staff assignments: infantry tactics instructor at West Point, Pentagon staff officer, and NATO plans officer. *The Harold G. Moore Collection*

Receiving a championship handball trophy for singles in the Fort Belvoir Handball Tournament. February 7, 1958. During his time in the Office of the Chief of Research and Development, Moore spent much of his leisure time playing handball. He often stressed that physical fitness helped maintain his mental awareness, a critical skill needed during the hectic days of Pentagon duty. He used to joke that he invented the sport of jogging; running in high top basketball shoes in the back roads near Fort Bragg, North Carolina and was even stopped once by the police who wanted to confirm he was not running from the scene of a crime. *The Harold G. Moore Collection*

Even in his later years, Moore routinely accepted physical challenges. In this picture, he stands with Russian veterans of their Afghan war on a Vietnam veterans outreach hike in 1988 through the pass in the mountains separating Uzbekistan from Kazakhstan. The Russians were amazed that a 66-year-old American General could keep up and, on the final day, several told him, "In the next war, we fight alongside you!" *The Harold G. Moore Collection*

Moore's children developed the same passion for physical fitness. While stationed in Norway, Steve and Greg (ages 8 and 9, respectively) would routinely ski by themselves along the trails surrounding Oslo. Both eventually earned the Norwegian Ski Association gold medal for skiing over 500 kilometers in a single winter. *The Harold G. Moore Collection*

LTC Hal Moore in his first command portrait as the CO of 2d Battalion, 23d Infantry. Moore's battalion was initially part of the 11th Air Assault Division, the first airmobile division in the US Army. The 11th Air Assault Division was later re-designated the 1st Cavalry Division (Airmobile). Moore's battalion then became the 1st Battalion, 7th Cavalry. *The Ballard Moore Collection*

Moore (left) stands alongside Sergeant Major Basil Plumley. Moore described him as an ornery, tough-as-nails NCO whose dedication and tenacity were second to none. Plumley epitomized the type of key advisor Moore would surround himself with. Moore ensured that Plumley understood his policies and expected him to be direct and candid if Moore was about to make a wrong decision *The Harold G. Moore Collection*

Moore (center) poses with his battalion officers prior to their deployment to Vietnam.
The Harold G. Moore Collection

Hal Moore and Sergeant Major
Basil Plumley outside the
battalion's base camp in South
Vietnam, October 1965. *The
Harold G. Moore Collection*

Soldiers at LZ X-Ray evacuate one of their wounded, November 15, 1965. *Joseph Galloway*

Moore and Plumley at the termite mound "command post" during the Battle of Ia Drang. Although greatly outnumbered, Moore never believed his unit would be defeated and communicated that confidence to his troopers. *The Harold G. Moore Collection*

For his audacious leadership and courage under fire during the Battle of Ia Drang, Hal Moore receives the Distinguished Service Cross from General William Westmoreland, the commander of American forces in Vietnam. *The Harold G. Moore Collection*

Following the battle at LZ X-Ray, Moore received his promotion to full Colonel and was given command of the 1st Cavalry Division's 3d Brigade. As a brigade commander, he led his troops through the high-profile Bong Son campaign of 1966. *The Harold G. Moore Collection*

Moore and his troops during OPERATION MASHER, January 1966. Moore routinely led from the front and shared the risks with his men. Larry Gwin wrote in his book, *Baptism*, that "I remember seeing Colonel Moore, the brigade commander. He was coming with us, on the ground. He was going to participate in the attack." The attack was on a bunker complex/trench line across open ground and occurred just a few days before Moore returned home. *Photo by Art Zich*

Moore confers with Captain Tony Nadal and another soldier during a "search-and-destroy" mission in Bong Son, 1966. *Photo by Art Zich*

From behind the menacing strands of concertina wire, Moore directs another helicopter sortie into the Central Highlands of Vietnam. *Look Magazine – Library of Congress*

Moore is promoted to Brigadier General on August 31, 1968 in a ceremony held at the Pentagon. Moore was the first member of his West Point class to be promoted to one-star, two-star, and three-star general. *The Harold G. Moore Collection*

Moore's command portrait as the commander of the 7th Infantry Division, then forward-stationed in the Republic of Korea. During his command tenure, Moore took great strides to correct the racial problems and rampant drug use throughout the division. *The Harold G. Moore Collection*

Moore gathers with the children of the Yang Ju Child Care Center. July 15, 1970. Moore's Division sponsored the Child Care Center as part of a public relations program to build better ties with the community. Thereafter, 7th Division soldiers were a regular sight at Yang Ju – reading stories to and playing games with the children. *The Harold G. Moore Collection*

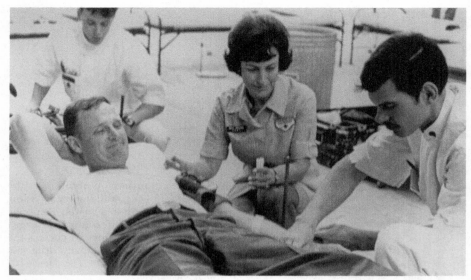

Hal Moore giving blood with the procedure supervised by Julie Moore. In addition to other volunteer work, Julie routinely served as a Red Cross volunteer. *The Harold G. Moore Collection*

The main entrance to Fort Ord, California during the early 1970s. Upon Hal Moore's return to the United States, he became the Commanding General of Fort Ord and the Army Training Center. *US Army photo*

General Moore and Command Sergeant Major Don Peroddy. Peroddy had been Moore's "right-hand man" during the latter's command of the 7th Infantry Division. Moore was so impressed by Peroddy and his handling of the NCOs, that Moore petitioned the Pentagon to ensure that Peroddy came with him to Fort Ord. Peroddy continued to serve as Moore's command sergeant major until 1973. *The Harold G. Moore Collection*

General Moore inspects the troops prior to a parade at Fort Ord, 1972. *The Harold G. Moore Collection*

Training on the M-60 Machine Gun. Heavy machine training was one of the many subjects Moore added to the Basic Training curriculum at Fort Ord. He hoped to create a program that would give all soldiers a strong foundation in infantry weapons and tactics, particularly given the nature of combat in Vietnam. *US Army photo*

Moore receives his third star on December 5, 1974. Following his promotion to Lieutenant General, Moore became the Army Deputy Chief of Staff for Personnel. *The Harold G. Moore Collection*

Moore's official portrait as the Deputy Chief of Staff for Personnel, 1975. Missing from his uniform is the Purple Heart awarded in Vietnam. Showing his respect for those who earned the medal at the price of their life, he wrote from Vietnam: "Please send me back that Purple Heart and award certificate. I cannot keep it as I feel that a minor punji stake wound to the foot is no reason... Although it was properly earned, I cannot wear it or keep it on conscience." *The Harold G. Moore Collection*

The semi-intact wreckage of the UH-1 helicopter upon which Moore was travelling during his observation of ROTC training at Fort Bragg, North Carolina, 1976. *The Harold G. Moore Collection*

An aerial view of the helicopter wreckage. The UH-1 had not ascended to more than 100 feet before experiencing engine trouble and crashing. Although the occupants (including Moore) sustained varying degrees of injury, all survived the crash. *The Harold G. Moore Collection*

Flight path of the ill-fated helicopter. *The Harold G. Moore Collection*

After retiring from the Army, Moore took a position as the Executive Vice President of the Crested Butte Mountain Resort in Colorado. He found the leadership principles that served him so well in the military were equally applicable to a civilian environment. *The Harold G. Moore Collection*

Like father, like son. Hal Moore and his son, Captain David Moore (left), attend a Veteran's Day celebration, 1991. David is wearing the Army's desert combat uniform, commemorating his recent service in the Persian Gulf War. The younger Moore went on to achieve the rank of Colonel, retiring in 2011 after nearly twenty-eight years of active service. *David Moore*

As part of the ABC Day One special, "They were Young and Brave," Moore returned to walk the Ia Drang battlefields with the North Vietnamese who fought against them. He developed a close friendship with his opposing commander, Lt. General Nguyen Huu An; each learning from the other how their individual decisions and actions impacted the fight. *The Harold G. Moore Collection*

Moore's combat helmet, worn during the gruesome three-day Battle of Ia Drang, displayed in silent reverence at his home in Auburn, Alabama. *Photo by author*

Moore and Plumley lead a procession of Ia Drang veterans at the Vietnam War Memorial during the 30th anniversary celebration of the battle. *Suzanne Sigona*

The human element of the Vietnam War Memorial. Statues frozen in time, gazing upon the names of their fallen comrades. *Photo by author*

Hal and Julie Moore at the Premiere showing of the 2002 Movie, *We Were Soldiers*. Both provided advice to the director, Randall Wallace, who had to caution them that he was not making a documentary. In the end, Hal and Julie were satisfied with the result. *The Harold G. Moore Collection*

Moore (second from left) receiving the Distinguished Graduate Award from West Point in 2003. Among his many other achievements, the citation notes, "Hal Moore's legacy is best summed up in the words of a former Chief of Staff of the Army: '...his greatest contribution has been his willingness to give of his life to teaching young officers and soldiers.'" *The Harold G. Moore Collection*

Moore met constantly with serving officers and soldiers; delivering innumerable presentations on leadership, ethics and the moral strength required to be successful. In those talks, he was never shy about addressing failures along with successes. *US Army*

Hal loved soldiers and believed one of his highest obligations was to mentor as many as he could. His special love was for the Non-Commissioned Officer and one of his proudest achievements was the work he led to rebuild an NCO corps destroyed by the Vietnam War. *The Harold G. Moore Collection*

Moore's Roman Catholic faith was his moral bedrock. He was grateful to the priests and deacons of his parish in Auburn, Alabama (St. Michael the Archangel Catholic Church) for providing ministry at his home when he was too infirm to attend Mass. *The Harold G. Moore Collection*

Perhaps the greatest validation of Moore's leadership ability and principles can be seen in the love his troopers had for him. When Moore was 94, 51 years after Vietnam, his troops took an afternoon out from their reunion to spend some time with him at his home. Moore tragically passed away on February 10, 2017 – just two days shy of his 95th birthday. *The Harold G. Moore Collection*

VIETNAM

Shortly after 9:00 a.m. on June 29, 1964, I was handed the colors of the 2nd Battalion, 23rd Infantry"—which had been detached from the 2d Infantry Division and assigned to the 11th Air Assault. "Accepting the Colors (Regimental flag with Battalion and Campaign streamers from earlier wars) means that the commander is now responsible *for all his command does or fails to do.*" Moore gave a brief talk to the 36 officers and 729 enlisted men of his new airmobile battalion. Standing in ranks on the parade ground at Kelly Hill, Fort Benning, he told his new charges: "We are a good battalion but we're going to get a lot better. Our goal is to be the best Air Assault Infantry Battalion in the 11th Air Assault Division. I will do my best. I expect the same from each of you."

Shortly before his change-of-command ceremony, Moore met the most memorable NCO of his career—Sergeant Major Basil L. Plumley. In Moore's own words, Plumley was "the very essence of an airborne soldier"—six foot two, square-jawed, with a crew cut and a penetrating stare." As a member of the 82d Airborne Division in World War II, he had participated in D-Day and Operation Market Garden. Since then, he had risen steadily through the ranks and was promoted to Sergeant Major in 1961. Moore instantly liked the man, but admitted the Sergeant Major "was very ornery." His imposing demeanor frequently scared the troops. Some even speculated that God himself looked like Sergeant Major Plumley. Nevertheless, Moore remarked there was no other command NCO whom he would rather have had by his side in Vietnam.

"When taking over an organization," Moore said, "you've got to stand out in front of your people, and state clearly what your goals are;

what you expect from them; and what they can expect from you. Then shut up and let everybody go to work. After the ceremony, I assembled my five company commanders, the six battalion staff officers, and the Battalion Sergeant Major to give them a word about my standards. They were straightforward:

- Only first place trophies will be displayed, accepted, or presented in this battalion. Get rid of all others immediately. Second place in our line of work is defeat on the battlefield. I am interested *only in winning*. So, it should be for any organization.

- Decision-making will be decentralized. It pays off on the battlefield.

- No fat troops or officers. In the military, physical fitness is paramount.

- I check up on everything.

- I am available day or night to talk to any officer of this battalion.

- Finally, the Sergeant Major works only for me and takes orders only from me. He is my right-hand man.

- It was an exciting time to be in the Airmobile Division. We were devising and testing new battlefield tactics. Electricity was in the air. Military leaders from across the world visited to see for themselves what was happening."

According to Hal Moore, General Kinnard was the perfect choice to lead the Army into the third dimension—free from what he called "the tyranny of terrain." Like Moore, Kinnard was a great believer in "pushing the power down." This was largely a function of his upbringing in the Airborne Divisions of World War II. "After a parachute assault into enemy territory," Moore said, "units would be scattered. Small unit leaders would be on their own." So, too, would it be on the air assault battlefield. Kinnard had done two combat jumps into Europe and, subsequently, "he wanted imaginative, aggressive commanders who thought fast and reacted quickly under pressure. He created an 'Idea Center' to which any man in his division could submit new ideas and concepts." This not only reinforced Hal's concept of mentoring, but it also taught him that:

> **A leader should surround himself with persons who fit his requirements and standards—and then turn them loose to do their jobs.**

"I was very fortunate to have two great mentors in those days;

my Brigade Commander, Col. Tim Brown and the Assistant Division Commander for Operations, Brigadier General Dick Knowles. They took me aside and advised me on Air Assault tactics and techniques. I was an apt pupil: I soaked it up, took notes, and took action. We were out in the field in Georgia and the Carolinas most of those fourteen months before Vietnam—maneuvering against other units, line infantry or paratroopers—such as troops of the 82nd Airborne Division."

At every turn, Moore continually emphasized pushing the power and decision-making authority down. "In battle," he said, "leaders are killed, or wounded and evacuated, and I made sure my company commanders and platoon leaders down the line were prepared for that by designating men under them to step up and take charge during a field exercise. I would often shout to a company commander or platoon leader: 'You've just been shot. *You're DEAD!* Now keep your mouth shut and watch what your men do—until I declare you back from the dead and back in action.'"

"In the large staff organizations and field commands I led, my policy was always to push the power down! If a subordinate staff officer, commander, or staff section leader felt comfortable and qualified to make a decision, he could do so with my authority and my responsibility. But, I made sure my people knew that I alone was responsible for what my staff or command did or failed to do. I am convinced my trust and loyalty downward resulted in better work habits and higher unit efficiency. That policy kept a hell of a lot of paperwork off my desk and gave me more time to think; to plan ahead, and to create the future. In the field, in battle, or training, that policy developed aggressiveness and took advantage of fast-moving openings to defeat the enemy. But most importantly, with such a policy, subordinates must be carefully informed by the boss regarding his views and guidance on what's going on, what are the priorities, policies, and principles in various situations. Many leaders are reluctant to delegate decision-making authority down to subordinates; by not doing so they keep a lot of monkeys on their backs—which eat up their time."

This concept is what Moore's sons named the "Rule of Doubts." Here is the full process:

- Every job has an implied or specified level of authority and responsibility. Use formally written job descriptions and personal counseling when on-boarding to ensure each individual understands the scope.

- When confronted with a decision, the individual asks themselves, "Does making this decision fall within my level of authority?" If so, the individual makes the decision. If not, he passes it up the chain of command.
- The next person in the chain of command reviews the issue and, if the decision should have been made at the lower level, he passes it back without action; forcing power down.
- Likewise, if the lower level decision should have been made at a higher level, the superior explains the reasons why to the subordinate to refine the subordinate's understanding of the scope of his authority.

Over a short period of time, this process clarifies, through practical application, each person's level of authority with the side effect of freeing the time of the senior leaders to focus on significant problems and not waste time dealing with issues that should have been resolved at a much lower level.

Moore's Observations, Lessons Learned or Re-learned:

- **It's a key responsibility of the leader, in any field of endeavor (athletic team, military, or business) to assure the successful continuity or ability of his organization to carry on should he die or become incapacitated. It's his duty to plan for such a contingency out of loyalty to his people and, if in a business endeavor, loyalty to his customers and, clients.**
- **Look for and find the really good "horses" in your organization and run them hard. Push them and challenge them with greater levels of responsibility.**
- **Leaders at all levels must know their stuff, be dead honest, have unquestioned personal integrity, set the example, and treat their people "fair and square."**
- **Strive for excellence, do not be content just to "get by."**
- **When confronted with a challenging problem, take a positive attitude. Face up to the facts and deal with them. Figure out a way to solve it.**
- **Select good people for your direct staff and make sure they know your policies. Instruct them not to hold back when they truly believe you are about to make a wrong decision.**
- **The key staff person is your Director of Operations. In other**

organizations he may be referred to as a Chief of Staff or Chief Operating Officer. He must be "inside your head." The relationship must be very close and very functional.

- Place emphasis on the importance physical exercise plays in improving mental acuity.

- Conduct fun, family-oriented events to enhance unit cohesion.

- Never take a subordinate to the woodshed in front of others; do that in private.

"In early July 1965, the colors of the 11th Air Assault Division were retired, and the Division was given the colors and designation of the 1st Cavalry Division (Airmobile). My battalion thus became the 1st Battalion, 7th Cavalry Regiment [1-7 Cavalry]"—the same ill-fated regiment commanded by Lieutenant Colonel George Armstrong Custer during the Battle of Little Bighorn. During the days of Custer's command, the regiment adopted the Irish drinking song "Garry Owen" as its marching tune. It soon became the official motto of the regiment and the men customarily greeted their officers with a salute and a cheery, "Garry Owen, Sir!"

Meanwhile, the situation in Vietnam had steadily gone from bad to worse. After winning their independence from the French in 1954, the resulting Geneva Conference separated Vietnam into two political entities: a northern zone, governed by the Communists, and a southern zone, which had become the Republic of Vietnam. Per the Geneva Accords, the Republic of Vietnam was to hold a reunification election in 1956. However, the South Vietnamese President, Ngo Dinh Diem, canceled the elections and vowed to stamp out any lingering Communists in the Republic of Vietnam. The Communists who remained in the south (the first incarnation of the Viet Cong) reciprocated by launching a low-level insurgency in 1957.

The US responded by increasing the footprint of its military advisory mission. By 1963, however, the insurgency had grown to a level that Washington could no longer ignore. Almost simultaneously, President Kennedy lost his confidence in Diem's ability to rule South Vietnam. On November 2, 1963, just weeks before Kennedy's own assassination, Ngo Dinh Diem was deposed and murdered in a coup d'état sanctioned and perhaps orchestrated by Washington, DC.

In the wake of Diem's assassination, however, Saigon went through a series of violent coups staged by South Vietnamese generals who took turns being "strongman of the month." Thus, with Diem out of the way and South Vietnam devolving into chaos, Hanoi felt the time had come to reunify Vietnam under Communist rule. By early 1965, as Communist incursions claimed the lives of more American servicemen, a frustrated President Johnson responded by sending the first combat troops into Vietnam. "By mid-September," Moore recalled, "the 1st Cavalry Division was in South Vietnam."

It was not without some resentment that Moore made his trip to Vietnam. When he assumed command of his battalion, it was nearly full-strength with 800 men. By the time the unit arrived on the battlefield at LZ X-Ray, it had less than 450. In fact, 1-7 Cavalry had suffered under the same dubious personnel policies plaguing the rest of the Army. President Johnson refused to declare a state of emergency or mobilize the Reserve or National Guard. Thus, any draftee or Reserve officer would not have their active duty tours extended to meet the deployment date. In fact, any soldier who was within sixty days of the end of his enlistment by August 1965 had to remain at Fort Benning. To make matters worse, when 1-7 Cavalry deployed to Vietnam, more than 100 troopers returned home when their enlistments expired that fall. It was a foolish move that took away Moore's most experienced men—the very soldiers who would be the most useful in combat.

"In late October, North Vietnamese Regulars attacked out of Cambodia into South Vietnam's Central Highlands. The 1st Cavalry Division was ordered to search for and destroy that enemy force. From November 14-16, my 450-man, under-strength battalion fought and defeated over 2,000 well-trained, aggressive soldiers of the 66th North Vietnamese Regiment. This was the first major battle of the war between US Army and PAVN [People's Army of North Vietnam] Regulars. It was fought around Landing Zone X-Ray in the Ia Drang Valley, six miles from the Cambodian border. It was a near non-stop battle—a fight that went down to the wire twice during those three days."

In fact, within a few hours of landing at LZ X-Ray, Moore's doomsday scenario had come to pass: his men were in heavy contact with the enemy *before* the rest of the battalion had arrived on the landing zone. To make matters worse, one of his platoons had been cut off and surrounded. That infamous "Lost Platoon" was led by Lieutenant Henry T. Herrick. Although Herrick was a gifted tactician, he was aggressive and bull-headed to the point of recklessness. Back at Fort Benning, Moore had considered giving Herrick command of the Reconnaissance Platoon, a coveted job among infantry lieutenants. When Moore mentioned the idea to Sergeant Major Plumley, however, his response was shocking: "Colonel, if you put Lieutenant Herrick in there, he will get them all killed." Moore was shocked that the new lieutenant had left such a bad impression on the Sergeant Major.

On another occasion, Herrick's own platoon sergeant, Sergeant First Class Carl Palmer, had confided to the company commander that the lieutenant's foolhardy aggressiveness might get the platoon killed. In fact, at Fort Benning, one of Herrick's men had drowned during a tactical river-crossing. According to Palmer, Herrick's heavy-handed aggression had been partly to blame. Today, however, the sergeant's dreadful prophecy would come true.

While maneuvering to reinforce another platoon, Herrick's men came across an enemy squad that quickly retreated upon their discovery. Herrick foolishly diverted his platoon to chase the enemy squad. Little did he realize, though, that he was leading his platoon right into an ambush. Within the hour, Lieutenant Herrick, Sergeant Palmer, and Sergeant Robert Stokes, the next ranking NCO, were killed in action. This left twenty-one-year-old Sergeant Ernie Savage to control the fight. Scrambling to save his battered platoon, Savage grabbed the radio and began calling artillery fire down on his position. For the next two days, Savage desperately clung to his rifle and his radio in the hopes of keeping the platoon alive. Beating back one enemy assault after another, Savage and the "Lost Platoon" were finally rescued by a relief force from Alpha Company.

The demise of Herrick's platoon highlighted one of Moore's leadership letdowns. *He failed to remove a toxic leader from the ranks.* In hindsight, the Sergeant Major's blunt assessment of Herrick, and the accidental drowning of his trooper, should have warranted Herrick's removal. Sergeant Palmer, a Korean War veteran, was certainly capable of taking the platoon into combat without the platoon leader. Perhaps Herrick could have been re-assigned to a staff section. Instead, the man whom two NCOs had pegged as a reckless leader was allowed to take his platoon into combat. Herrick's soldiers ultimately paid the price. Had Palmer been in charge, the "Lost Platoon" may never have been. In the end, toxic leaders always do more harm than good. The leadership lesson here is:

When you identify a toxic subordinate leader, remove them. If you cannot remove them, reassign them to a role where their toxicity can be minimized.

Notwithstanding Herrick and his fatal mistake, the men of 1-7 Cavalry more than held their own against a numerically-superior force. "I fleetingly thought about a previous commander of the 7th Cavalry," Moore said, "Lieutenant Colonel George Armstrong Custer, and his last stand at Little Big Horn in Montana. I was determined that history would not repeat itself in the Ia Drang Valley in Vietnam. And never did it cross my mind that we might go down. *I knew we would prevail.*

"On the third day," Moore recalled, "the enemy quit the battlefield and retreated to his sanctuary in Cambodia—leaving over 600 dead and their weapons littering the field. I lost 79 killed, 121 wounded, none missing. For those interested in the military details, read the book *We Were Soldiers Once...and Young* written by Joseph Galloway and myself. I am compelled, however, to make a few observations:

- During the X-Ray battle, my great troopers and I *never quit*. The extension of that lesson is that a unit—be it military, an athletic team, a business organization, or a political organization—takes on and reflects the personality of the boss, the commander, the coach... *the leader.*

- As I stated in the first chapter, one of my Four Basic Principles of Leadership is *trust your instincts*. An example from the X-Ray battle occured at around 2:00 p.m. on November 14, 1965. Only two of my four companies (totaling approximately 190 men) were on the ground. We were up against nearly 1,000 North Vietnamese who were fiercely determined to overrun and kill us all. My whole rear was open as I had no men to place there. When the lead elements of Captain Bob Edwards' Charlie Company landed by helicopter, I ran out to Edwards and hollered at him to 'Run your men towards the mountain, tie in with Alpha Company on your right and get ready to be attacked in strength. MOVE!' He sped off where I pointed with his 106 men. Within minutes they were in hasty defensive positions in the tree line. Ten minutes later, a wave of 500 North Vietnamese slammed into them. The enemy was surprised and ultimately repelled in a fierce 45-minute battle. Had I sent Edwards and his men in any other direction, that fresh North Vietnamese unit would have had a clear shot at the rear of my force and would have owned the Landing Zone. *Instincts.* Every instinct I had told me to send Edward's men where I did. In a fast-moving situation, the leader must *trust his instincts.*

- When a member of a unit (military or non-military) loses his life, or when a member has a death in the family, it's the duty of the leader to take sincere action in expressing personal condolences, sympathy or any other appropriate steps considering the circumstances.

- When a large number of any unit are killed, such as the air crash involving the US Figure Skating Team or the 9/11 World Trade Center murders, far more actions are required of a leader. That was my situation in late November 1965 after the Ia Drang Battle. We were a family team, now stricken with grief, and vulnerable to being sent back into battle—which we were within a month. You do whatever you can to ease the pain of the men in the combat zone and for the next-of-kin back home, to help morale, and reduce the shock and terrible truth of it all. In civilian tragedies such as those cited above, the same leadership actions are required of civilian leaders. In this respect, Rudy Giuliani, the Mayor of New York City is a stellar, historic example.

- Regarding relations with the news media: During the first night of the X-Ray Battle, a radio message came to me that Joe Galloway, a 23-year-old UPI war correspondent, wanted my permission to fly in on a re-supply helicopter. I approved it. I had known Joe for only four days. He'd joined one of my companies on a combat patrol on November 10 and spent the night with us, cold and wet, in the mountainous jungle instead of hitching a ride in a chopper back to Pleiku for a shower and hot food. I liked that. Besides, I wanted the American people to know what my great troopers were doing in that war. Joe stayed with us, under fire, for the rest of that battle and did indeed tell the world about that fight, my men, and the fierce enemy we had defeated. For the rest of my time in Vietnam, I welcomed reporters and permitted the news media to accompany my units into battle. I had only two restrictions: (1) Do not interfere with on-going operations; (2) Do not release any information that will endanger us.

"My experience during the military and afterwards in business showed me there are at least two categories of 'what ifs' in any endeavor: *those that you can do something about and those you cannot.* Either way, it is a grave mistake not to plan for them. Be ready.

"I was never comfortable taking a lot of risks that were out of my control or could have disastrous consequences if a situation went sour. On the battlefield, when taking a bold risk, my staff and I carefully calculated it with detailed forethought not only to make it work, but to think through contingency plans regarding what we would do if we ran into trouble. It is imperative to have a plan to follow through so you can exploit success when you are blessed with it.

"A common theme running through books and stories about leaders is they made sure they knew what the pitfalls and negatives were. But rather than fretting and worrying about them, they calculated how to avoid or defeat them. As Sun Tzu, the great Chinese scholar, wrote in the fourth century BC, 'Know your enemy and know yourself: and in a hundred battles you will never be in peril.' On the business battlefields that principle could be paraphrased: 'Know your competition, know your capabilities, know your market, know yourself and you will succeed.'"

"Despite detailed preparation, when events do not go as planned, when you are sideswiped by adversity, face up to the facts and deal with them. No whining; no 'if only.' You can't change the facts, but there is always one more thing you can do to influence any situation in your favor. There's always a way!

"You can read those leadership and management books until the cows come home or until Hell freezes over, but if you want it boiled down, good leadership revolves around good *judgment*. That is the defining characteristic of a good leader. Some think that character is the key to leadership, with its implication of strict adherence to a rigid code of ethics, integrity, honesty, personal morals, mental strength, and toughness. I disagree. If a leader has good judgment, he or she already has the character and integrity to choose the harder right over the easier wrong. Yet you can have character and integrity and still exercise bad judgment. How?

"Any of these ills—incomplete or wrong information, stress, a tired mind, a weary body, poor advice, ignoring sound advice, personal ego or pride, or a poor analysis of the situation—can push a leader of character and integrity over the line into bad judgment.

"Most historians agree that General Robert E. Lee was a leader of the highest character and integrity. But his poor judgment in ordering Pickett's division to charge across a half mile of open fields into the entrenched guns of the Union Army resulted in a terrible slaughter of his soldiers and General Lee's defeat at Gettysburg. The general, after the disaster, offered his resignation. That exhibited his character and integrity but did not excuse his bad judgment."

"I've always been keenly interested in why leaders fail. I learned early in my career to have a trusted confidant with broad experience, sagacity, and wisdom close at hand. As I moved up, I always tried to find such a person and put him directly under me as my operations officer, chief of staff, or special assistant. I wanted someone who was loyal enough to me and the unit to be the 'skunk at the picnic'—to tell me candidly when he thought I was about to go off on a wrong tangent. Sometimes I agreed; sometimes not. But that was the essence of loyalty to me, to the unit, and to the mission. General Lee had such a loyal advisor, Gen. James Longstreet, who strongly advised against sending Pickett's division on that suicidal charge, but Lee rejected that advice. When I was a battalion and brigade commander in Vietnam, my loyal advisor, my sounding board, was my S-3, or operations officer, Captain Greg "Matt" Dillon. It was the voices of Dillon and Sergeant Major Plumley I listened to as we prepared and planned the assault into LZ X-Ray. Once we were engaged in the decisive battle, there was little time for further discussion; only the hard, lonely duty of command."

But the horrific battle nonetheless took its toll on Moore. "If there was one moment on the battlefield that was the worst of it all," he said, "it came in victory." He had won the first major battle of the Vietnam War, "but 79 of my precious men had gone down. I was on the ground trying to come to grips with our terrible loss of men. Joe Galloway kneeled with me. I told him:

'I'll never forgive myself.'

Joe responded, 'For what, sir?'

'That my men died and I didn't.'

"Before and after 1965, my life as a soldier was utterly different. Before 1965, those were the days of learning as if I would live forever—that I was bulletproof. After 1965, those were the days of learning from others and living every day knowing full well it might be my last."

What made the difference in that battle, according to Moore, "was the will of my troopers to win, their unit discipline, and teamwork. Here's an example. During the second night, Sergeant John Setelin, was wounded in one of his arms by burning White Phosphorous. He used the point of his bayonet to dig burning fragments out of his flesh. The enemy attacked again and he went back to firing his rifle, ignoring his smoking arm. An hour later, after the attack had been defeated, Setelin went to the aid station."

With his arm bandaged, he was waiting to be evacuated on the next medical chopper before he realized that he could not, in good conscience, leave the battlefield while his squad mates remained in the fight. Setelin promptly took off his sling and walked away from the aid station. When asked where he was going, Setelin casually replied, "back to my foxhole."

Moore cited this example because it showcased Setelin's "strong sense of responsibility and duty," and it illustrated "the eternal truth that it's the people down in the ranks who get the job done. I emphasized to my men that:

> **_Their_ duty at _their_ level was just as important
> as _my_ duty at _my_ level.**

This is true in any organization. The grunts who do the dog work are absolutely essential to success."

On November 23, 1965, Moore was promoted to full Colonel. "Shortly thereafter," he said, "General Kinnard gave me command of the Division's 3rd Brigade. In this capacity, I commanded anywhere from 2,000 to 4,000 men. We were involved in six different operations over the next six months, spanning the unpopulated, jungle borders of Laos and Cambodia to the densely populated, rice-growing regions along the South China Sea."

Throughout 1966, the coastal campaigns received plenty of attention from the American media. Publications such as _Time, Newsweek,_ and the various men's adventure magazines ran stories on Moore and his tactical leadership in Vietnam. In February 1966, a headline in the Detroit Free Press labeled Moore as "Vietnam War's George Patton." The article opened by asking a wounded soldier clutching his shattered arm on a medivac what he thought of Moore. "I'd go anywhere with that SOB," was the simple response. But whereas General Patton was gruff and bombastic, Moore was the quiet and measured professional. Still, the parallels of success were hard to ignore. Both men rallied their troops to surprising victories by leading from the front.

Leaders lead from the front; managers lead from the rear.

Hal Moore drew inspiration from "Old Blood and Guts" Patton. "Before Vietnam," he said, "I had read a lot of military history and was deeply impressed by the leadership of Field Marshal Erwin Rommel and General George S. Patton, Jr. Their style emphasized four bedrock principles:

1. Surprise

2. Aggressiveness

3. Deception

4. The leader's personal presence in the battle.

They were very helpful to me on the battlefields of Vietnam."

Of the sudden press coverage, however, Moore said, "Immediately after the battle [at LZ X-Ray], my every move seemed to be watched by the media. For the first year after the battle, I hoped things would die down, but they did not. It only grew with intensity, and the press wouldn't leave me alone. On December 5, 1966, in *Newsweek*, with Westmoreland on the cover and me with others on the inside, the press kept coming. This was most uncomfortable and certainly unworthy. All I ever wanted to be was a soldier, find the enemy, and do what I had pledged to the commander-in-chief that I would do. Daily reports would come out from the news services about what my troopers had done the day before. My personality was being described in the press and my troopers were being asked questions about my leadership style. In certain circles, I was spoken about as a 'hero' of sorts. This was most unfair and not true, for I had trained the heroes—and they were my troopers." This extract from a letter Moore wrote to his wife on March 3, 1966, was typical of his continuing complaint about personal publicity at the expense of covering the unit and troops. "I am hoping the publicity will die down in reference to me. I prefer for my men and the unit's accomplishments to get it, not me... I hope correspondents will stay away from me."

Still, the American press corps couldn't help themselves. One feature story in June 1966 described Moore as follows:

"To his soldiers, he is Daniel Boone, Wild Bill Hickok, James Bond, Teddy Roosevelt, and William Tecumseh Sherman all rolled into six feet of bone-hard Kentuckian.'"

Flattering as it was, this headline highlighted the effectiveness of Moore's leadership. For even in the deadliest of battles, whatever the risk, Moore *always* led from the front. On February 1, 1966, Moore was with a rifle company when it became heavily engaged with the enemy.

A portion of his Bronze Star for Valor citation states Moore, "bravely moved forward through the enemy's withering small arms and automatic weapons fire out into the open field to one seriously wounded soldier, and carried him over fifty meters to safety." Around this time, Hal's troops began calling him "One More Moore," as he always seemed to have one more fight in him.

A sergeant remarked, "Lots of commanders are always complaining that they take their men into the field and then they can't find the enemy. They've disappeared in tunnels or something. But when you're under Moore's command, you know damn well you're in for action. And you're gonna win." A more senior NCO characterized Moore as a gambler. "But like good gamblers," he said, "he knows his cards and when to play 'em, when to raise, and when to fold his hand. You know, everybody in Vietnam is talking about the need for a real colorful leader to emerge from this war. A Patton-type leader, who can inspire the men with courage and brains instead of the human computers that the Ivy League ROTCs turn out. If this war lasts any longer, and it looks that way, they'll find out they got one that ranks with the best of 'em—and he's under their noses—commanding the Third Brigade right now."

On another occasion, Moore was traveling with the lead element of a patrol when he came across some of his troops getting ready to throw a hand grenade into a bunker on the outskirts of a nearby village. Realizing the operation was taking place near a populated area, Moore feared there may have been women and children hiding within the bunker complex. He instructed his men to use a smoke grenade instead. Drawing from his experience in Occupied Japan, Moore remembered that one of his fellow officers had playfully thrown a smoke grenade into the Bachelor Officer Quarters at Camp Crawford. And, just as it had done in Japan, the smoke grenade cleared out the bunker within a matter of seconds. True to his hunch, a frightened posse of Vietnamese women and children emerged from the bunker, screaming and coughing, but otherwise unharmed. Although the smoke grenade was a heavy-handed tactic, Moore knew that it was better to positively identify the occupants of the bunker before engaging it with deadly fire.

Eventually, more than 9,000 air cavalrymen participated in the coastal campaigns of 1966. Hal Moore's brigade killed 893 enemy troops and took more than 300 enemy prisoners of war. "I lost 82 KIA, 318 WIA, and none missing. In two wars, I was very proud that I never had a man captured or reported missing in action." Moore was less impressed, however, with the aftermath of the fighting. "After clearing the area of

Viet Cong, we turned the area over to the ARVN [Army of the Republic of Vietnam] and South Vietnamese government officials, and the enemy was back within seven days."

"Although I was a battlefield commander," he said, "and not involved in the politics of it all, it was evident to me that if the Vietnamese military and government couldn't keep even a small area under control, how could they possibly control all of South Vietnam?" Lesson learned:

When the battle is over, there must be plans (made in advance) for follow-on actions.

After leaving Vietnam in July 1966, Moore returned to Washington DC, where he spent a year in the Office of the Under Secretary of Defense. As the "Military Liaison to the Assistant Secretary for International Affairs," his primary duties were creating "Trip Books" for senior officials visiting Vietnam and drafting replies to what he called "Congressionals," or "letters [about] Vietnam from the constituents of Senators and Congressmen."

From these letters, it was clear the country was growing more restless over the war in Vietnam. Amidst the ongoing public backlash, Moore realized the American people were becoming increasingly hostile towards the military. To make matters worse, many had resorted to blaming the military for its involvement in the war. The same US servicemen who had been heralded as "heroes" in 1965 were now being called "baby killers."

"As stated in Galloway's and my book, for the next year I watched Bob McNamara [Secretary of Defense] and John McNaughton [Assistant Secretary of Defense for International Security Affairs], both brilliant men, go through hell as they struggled unsuccessfully to get a handle on the war in Vietnam. By the end of that year, neither of them were any closer to finding or creating such a handle." In fact, during a 1967 Department of Defense briefing, one senior officer sadly and succinctly told them what was happening in Vietnam: "Although we have redoubled our efforts, we have lost sight of our objective."

Years later, while reflecting on the war in Vietnam, Moore offered this, "The whole Vietnam generation numbered 53.1 million. Three million served in Vietnam. The average age was 19 years. 7,484 were women. Two-thirds of those Americans volunteered for Vietnam, a little-known fact. 321,000 casualties. More than 2,000 still unaccounted for. 75,000 crippled for life. In that parade of the dead on the long black wall in Washington are 58,229 names, including 8 women nurses. Their deeds for America, for their fellow soldiers, and for the cause of freedom are history. All those men and women who were sent 12,000 miles to fight, to serve, to die in that unintelligible, no-win war were not in Tom Brokaw's 'Greatest Generation,' but they were surely the greatest of their generation. On the battlefield, soldiers do not fight and die for the flag, the country, or for what a President says on TV. Soldiers in battle fight for each other, they kill for each other, and they die for each other."

"Finally, even though it cost the lives of more than 58,000 young Americans, and inflicted humiliating defeat on a nation that had never before lost a war, some of us learned that Carl von Clausewitz had it right 150 years earlier when he wrote these words: *'No one starts a war— or rather, no one in his sense ought to do so—without first being clear in his mind what he intends to achieve by the war and how he intends to conduct it.'"*

For Hal Moore, the Clausewitz quote underscored the fundamental problem with Vietnam. "From 1964 until the American withdrawal in 1973, our objectives kept changing: from political stability and preventing an enemy takeover to preserving the independence of South Vietnam and training ARVN forces. At first, the US pushed the South Vietnamese Army aside and took over the war with a brand of fighting that only American forces and American logistics could support. When we left in 1973, our heritage was just that, a form of war that South Vietnam and its armed forces could not sustain."

"In the late 1970s, the Army Chief of Military History, General Douglas Kinnard, wrote a book called *The War Managers*. He sent a questionnaire to 175 Army generals who had served in Vietnam. His book is an analysis of their replies. Nearly seventy percent of those generals were uncertain and unclear as to what the US objective was in Vietnam!" For Moore, it reinforced the idea that:

A leader must have clearly defined objectives.
He must ensure that these objectives are
clearly understood by his subordinate leaders.

Reflecting on the misadventure in Vietnam, Moore offered the following rules of thumb for any leader considering sending troops into combat:

1. The President should not commit military forces into a foreign country unless US national interests or national security are directly involved or threatened.

2. If military forces are committed, the commander should be given a clearly-defined, doable mission.

3. The commitment should be supported by a majority of the American people.

4. There must be a feasible military plan to accomplish the mission.

5. There should be a clearly defined exit strategy.

"None of these lessons," he said, "were heeded during the tragic military adventure in Somalia, in Haiti, and were not factors in the commitment of thousands of US military forces into Bosnia and Kosovo. They were certainly not factors in the lead-up to the Iraq War."

In 1968, Moore was promoted to Brigadier General—the first of his West Point classmates to achieve flag rank. He then returned to the Pentagon where he spent 10 months working for the Deputy Chief of Staff for Operations (DCSOPS). At DCSOPS, Moore said, "I supervised planning for the withdrawal of American ground troops from Vietnam." By now, President Johnson's turnabout on Vietnam had morphed into President Nixon's policy of "Vietnamization"—a redeployment of American combat forces while training the South Vietnamese to take the lead in the fighting.

"In July 1969, I was sent to the Headquarters of the Eighth US Army in Seoul, Korea." Reporting to General Charles H. Bonesteel, the commander of the United States Forces Korea (USFK), Moore became "the Plans and Operations Officer, the G-3, of the Eighth Army in Korea. I was a brigadier general on the two-star list." From his new office in Seoul, Moore remarked that "I visited with military units on the front lines of the Demilitarized Zone [DMZ] to check on the defense plans and to get to know the terrain, roads, and the principal commanders." But as Moore soon found out, the Republic of Korea wasn't the best place to be in 1969.

SUMMARY

A leader should surround himself with persons who fit his requirements and standards—and then turn them loose to do their jobs.

When you identify a toxic subordinate leader within your ranks, remove them. If you cannot remove them, reassign them to a role where their toxicity can be minimized.

Their duty at *their* level was just as important as *my* duty at *my* level.

Leaders lead from the front; managers lead from the rear.

When the battle is over, there must be plans (made in advance) for follow-on actions.

A leader must have clearly defined objectives. He must ensure these objectives are clearly understood by his subordinate leaders.

THE GUIDING HAND

In the summer of 1969, the DMZ was one of two frontiers in America's Cold War—the other being the Inner-German Border, the largest swath of the "Iron Curtain." Sixteen years earlier, the Korean War had ended in a cease-fire. As a result of the 1953 armistice, the US kept a permanent military presence along the DMZ to deter any further aggression from North Korea. On October 1, 1969, General Bonesteel relinquished his command of USFK to General John H. Michaelis, who had been the Commandant at West Point when Moore was an Infantry Tactics Instructor.

As Moore described him, Michaelis was "a very demanding taskmaster. General Michaelis would fire a subordinate on the spot if he were displeased with that officer's performance on a task or in a job—no second chance." To stay ahead of a boss like that, or any boss, Moore offered the following:

- Know your stuff and work your tail off.

- Early on, study the boss carefully. Talk to others who have worked for him. Determine his primary interests. Listen. *Take notes*. Take every opportunity to keep your mouth shut around him except to answer a question or to tell him something important he should know. Never let him get surprised by information that you should have alerted him about earlier. Stay on top of his primary interests.

- Always get to the workplace before the boss. Read up on what's happened overnight. If a crisis or situation has occurred in which the boss will be involved, notify him quickly. If it's a matter on which you have the authority to act and are *comfortable* in doing so, DO IT!

- Know your territory. If your boss supervises a lot of units or work places, take the time to get out from behind your desk and visit with the subordinate supervisors and workers. Talk with them. See for yourself (and your boss) their working conditions, their morale, their needs, and the efficiency of their workplace. See if there are any festering problems which can be nipped in the bud. See if there are any opportunities or new ideas that should be exploited by YOUR BOSS. See if any persons should be recognized for outstanding performance or any subordinate supervisor your boss should talk to regarding improvements.

- There are at least five activities that must be kept in balance through proper time management. This is not easy for a busy executive with significant responsibilities, especially in this world of "information overload." These five activities are: the job, physical fitness, personal time alone, recreation, and social relationships. Also, if they apply, two others—religion and family. If any of these get out of balance, then life gets out of balance. From my own personal experience and observation of others, being a workaholic is the most common area of imbalance.

During his visits to the DMZ, aside from getting to know the terrain and meet local commanders, Moore would also check to ensure General Michaelis' orders were being carried out. "I was in my office by 5:45 a.m. six days a week—on Sunday mornings also until time to take my family to church." However, to Hal Moore, it seemed that keeping the boss satisfied was the least of his worries.

"During the later Vietnam War years of 1969–1971," he said, "Korea was a hotbed of racial tensions and heavy drug use. These were the days of…marijuana, all colors of pills with a lot of Koreans making their living selling these to American soldiers. Houses of prostitution and bars were outside the gates of all military bases and did a booming business. Altercations between black and white soldiers were frequent."

Suddenly, the racial tensions in Korea exploded late one night in May 1970. On that night, Moore said, "the 7th Division [headquartered at Camp Casey along the DMZ] experienced a number of fights between black soldiers, white soldiers, and Hispanic soldiers. It was a major brawl that lasted all night." Shortly after midnight, Moore was awakened by his staff duty officer with an alarming report that the barracks had been trashed and several buildings were on fire, "including," Moore said, "the Post Library." In fact, the situation had gotten so out of control that the MPs had to call on the local Korean police for assistance.

Meanwhile, Moore leapt out of bed and raced to his office. Although it was nearly 2:00 a.m. the entire Eighth Army Headquarters was swarming with staff officers—all frantically taking calls and riffling through various reports trying to get a handle on the situation at the DMZ. "It was just after 8:00 a.m.," Moore recalled, when his desk "squawk box" buzzed. The voice on the other end said, "General Michaelis wants to see you immediately." Moore ran up the stairs and reported to his boss.

Michaelis wasted no time. "Moore, you know what's happened in the 7th Division. It's in a hell of a shape. I've relieved the Division Commander. I've gotten permission from Washington to frock you with your second star," meaning that Moore would become a two-star general with the pay of a one-star until his official promotion date. Michaelis then gave Hal simple instructions: "I want you to get up there and straighten out that goddamned division!"

"Yes sir," Moore replied. "When do I leave?"

"In half an hour."

"The 7th Infantry Division was a typical division," Hal said, "draftees mostly." He felt a special connection to the unit, having served as a Regimental S-3 and company commander with the division during some of the bloodiest battles in the Korean War. Now, the division consisted of some 16,000 men and officers scattered across twenty-three camps in South Korea. Outside the Division Headquarters at Camp Casey was the village of Dongduchon, where American GIs frequented its bars, drug houses, and brothels.

"I won't go into all the details on the actions I took, as they would not all be of interest to the non-military leader. But I will mention a few that are translatable to the civilian world:

- In a big outfit, a large organization, some units will be in excellent shape, some less so. Some will have good leaders, some less so. Some will have persons in the ranks, people who are troublemakers, or inefficient or are a negative influence on the workplace. Some will have workers who should be rewarded with recognition, promotion, more authority, or responsibility, but have not been because of poor leadership. And so it was in the 7th Infantry Division. The officers, NCOs, and the troops in the ranks were rightfully curious about their new commander and how he would tackle the situation.

- When an organization is beset with problems, and a new boss is brought in to shape it up, the new boss should not assume the entire organization has those problems. He should, however, take quick action to stop the problems from spreading. In so doing, he must be careful not to cause the good, well-performing units to get the erroneous impression that the boss is 'coming down' on *them*. He should quickly determine which sub-units are in trouble and which are not and take appropriate action. This also requires a hard look at the leadership in those units."

This philosophy was absolutely the right prescription. When beset with cultural problems in an organization, the leader must be careful not to lump everyone into the same category. Moore's new program of discipline was exactly what the unit needed, but he knew if he treated the entire division like a gang of misfits, it would backfire on him. The mantra was simple:

A leader should never tell an outfit that it's screwed up.
If he does, then it will be screwed up.
Why? Because the boss said so.

Remember, a unit's performance and morale often reflect the attitude of its leadership. In the case of the 7th Infantry Division, Moore knew that the unit was aware of its own deficiencies. Bludgeoning them with lectures would not earn their confidence or respect. Instead, he complimented the division on the things it did well—and candidly told them where they needed to improve. This holds true for any leader in any organization:

If you seek to correct a subordinate's overall behavior or performance, start by telling them what they do well, then tell them where they need to improve.

This approach inspires loyalty within the subordinate while maintaining their self-respect. Furthermore, it lets them know that the boss values their contributions, appreciates their strengths, and is not merely on the lookout for deficiencies.

"In any case," he said, "the new Top Brass should not just drift in, take over a desk, and start reading the paperwork. The first thing a new boss has to do is stand up in front of every person in the unit; let his people see him. He should visit each sub-unit personally and strongly impress his personality and spirit on the subordinate leaders and workers in the ranks. Concurrently, he should learn his responsibilities and what each of his subordinate units is charged with accomplishing."

Over a 10-day period, Moore flew his helicopter to each of his camps in South Korea and talked for fifteen minutes or so to every unit in the division. "Since the biggest problem facing me was the highly flammable racial situation, my top priority was to get that cooled down and under control. My principal message was that I would see to it that every man would be treated fair and square and it was up to every man to rise as far as his abilities would take him. To deal with these racial tensions, I first had to get the facts on the details and scope of the problem. This I did on the highest priority. Right off, I learned if there were perceived problems of unfair discrimination, those *perceptions* had to be dealt with just as carefully as *real* problems—and with just as high a priority.

"I quickly located the units with problems and promptly took corrective action with both the commanders and the troublemakers—white, black, or brown. Many were discharged. Early on, it was evident to me that many of the race relations problems, perceptions and real cases of discrimination occurred at the small unit level. As I checked into that, the other small-unit leadership deficiencies came to light." To correct these problems at the small-unit level, Moore instituted an Officer's Leadership School for company-grade officers and an NCO Leadership School for staff sergeants and below. Each course was a week long (Sunday–Saturday) and taught by instructors carefully selected from across the division. Moore himself even taught a few of these courses. "These schools went a long way toward reducing the racial and drug abuse problems."

Around this time, Hal Moore issued his Equal Opportunity Policy:

"People are our most important asset in the 7th Infantry Division. In all that we do, each person must be recognized as an individual; recognizing his aspirations, capabilities, and personal needs. Each man must be continually provided fair treatment and equal opportunity, within appropriate regulations, to rise as high a level of responsibility as his talent and diligence will take him."

He knew he couldn't change racial attitudes on his own, but he could make it a punishable offense for a leader to discriminate based on race or ethnicity.

"Acting on experience and from past study of successful commanders, I instituted really tough day-and-night training, various numerous off-duty high school/college skills classes, and all kinds of athletic team competitions. We won the Eighth Army football championship, the boxing championship, and the basketball championship. Bus trips to historical Korean War battlefields were organized. Very high standards of individual and unit discipline were established and enforced." Reaching out to the local community, Moore also had the division sponsor the nearby Yang Ju Child Care Center. For the remainder of his command, 7th Division soldiers were a regular sight among the children; playing games, giving out food, and even teaching English.

During this time, Moore recalled that: "I had two principal advisers. Colonel Jack Bishop was a three-war Infantry veteran who began his military service in the California National Guard as a private, age sixteen. He'd risen through the ranks, knew all the moves, had heard all the stories, and experienced most of the problems. He was my chief of staff—dead loyal, dead honest, and very candid. The other was the senior non-commissioned officer in the division—Command Sergeant Major Don Peroddy, a tough fireplug of a man who wore a handful of Purple Hearts and Silver Stars from Vietnam. He worked only for me, took orders only from me, and had unlimited access to me day or night. He ran the NCOs of the division; set the standards, checked up on them, and was fearless. My first order to him: 'Sergeant Major, I don't want any more problems in the villages around our camps. No more fights. No more problems with the Koreans.' He straightened things out fast and kept them straight with NCOs in the bars and on the streets working with the military police. Early every morning and late every afternoon, I met with each of those men, and we talked about immediate problems, developing situations, and whatever they or I wanted to bring up."

Moore's Observations, Lessons Learned or Relearned:

- **The boss in any organization needs one or two trusted, proven advisors.**

- **I kept in shape by running four miles every morning early before breakfast and, during bad weather, by playing handball late in the afternoon. My goal, which I continually expressed to my officers and men, was for the 7th Division to be the best division in the Army; to be prepared to take to the field on a no-notice basis to defend South Korea. They were frequently reminded that the war in Korea was *not* over—it had not ended; there was only an armistice.**

By the end of Moore's command tenure, the division's disciplinary problems had virtually disappeared, and combat readiness surged to an all-time high. However, in the spring of 1971, the Army was ordered to deactivate one of its divisions in Korea. At the time, only two infantry divisions were forward-stationed along the DMZ: the 2nd Infantry Division and the 7th Infantry Division. Ironically, even considering Moore's remarkable performance in turning around the 7th Division, the Army selected it for deactivation. "The 2nd Infantry Division would remain," he recalled wryly. "This meant I had to thoroughly clean and close down most of my camps and stations. Others would be turned over to the 2nd Division or the South Korean Army along with all of our tanks, trucks, weapons, etc. My officers and troops would receive orders to report elsewhere. This we did, and in April 1971 our colors were cased."

Departing Korea, Moore took on a new assignment as the Post Commander and Commandant of the Army Training Center in Fort Ord, California. Nestled at the edge of Monterey Bay, and within driving distance of San Francisco, Ord was one of the most sought-after assignments in the Army. It was the hub of the Fort Ord Military Complex which included the nearby Presidio of Monterey and Fort Hunter Liggett approximately eight miles to the south.

"Fort Ord was an infantry training center," Moore said, "where thousands of recruits were put through several months of Basic and Advanced Infantry Training. It was a city of over 50,000 with hundreds of Army families in government housing. There were schools, clubs, two golf courses, a football stadium, gymnasiums, shopping facilities, a large hospital, a stockade (military prison), an airfield with Army helicopters and small fixed-wing aircraft, and a lot of vehicular traffic. The Presidio of Monterey was a very small post on which the Army Language School was located. Fort Hunter Liggett sprawled across thousands of acres where developmental army vehicles and weapons were tested.

"My boss was Lt. General Stanley R. 'Swede' Larsen, Commanding General of the 6th US Army." Like Moore, Larsen was also a West Pointer— Class of 1939. During World War II, Larsen had earned the Distinguished Service Cross for actions in the Pacific. He had also been the personal aide to Army Chief of Staff General J. Lawton Collins during the Korean War, and later commanded the 10th Infantry Division in West Germany. "His headquarters was 125 miles north in the Presidio of San Francisco. After arriving in California by plane from Korea, I reported to General Larsen. We knew each other from Vietnam, five years earlier." Larsen had commanded American ground forces within the II Corps Tactical Zone of Vietnam. "He sat me down in his office and gave me a wealth of helpful guidance on my new command. He had commanded Fort Ord several years earlier. *Mentoring*! From his experience, his leadership proved to be right on the mark.

"My primary activity was training infantry recruits and running Fort Ord. Nearby were the cities of Monterey, Seaside, Salinas, Carmel, and Pacific Grove. Although recruits in training were not allowed off-post, several of my officers, NCOs and their families lived in these cities." Moore also remembered that the Army fed a lot of money into the economy of Northern California, including contracts for construction and renovation, as well as revenue from numerous visitors attending the recruits' graduation. Observing these dynamics, his lessons were clear:

- A leader, after taking over an organization and setting his standards, must do a thorough "Estimate of the Situation" in his organization. The purpose is to reveal problem areas, opportunities, and areas of excellence.

- Wherever there's a large business organization (or a large military installation) and a city or town in the same general area, it's very helpful for all parties to develop and maintain healthy relationships as they interact with each other.

"I joined the Monterey Rotary Club, attended the weekly lunch meetings when possible, and became acquainted with numerous business leaders. Some of my senior officers joined other civic clubs in Monterey, Salinas, and Seaside. We became acquainted with the local mayors and city managers. We paid particular attention to establishing good relations with the local police and arranged for my several troop commanders (fifteen or so) to be on a roster to ride along in local police cars at night."

In the spirit of building better ties with the local community, Moore put together several "activity days" where civilians could come and observe Basic Training. He invited many community leaders and journalists from nearby cities to "see where the troops lived, eat with the troops, even talk with the soldiers privately. I welcomed the reporters in particular and saw to it that they could go anywhere they wanted and talk with anyone on post." His only stipulation was that they not interfere with training.

"When I took command in April 1971," he said, "drafted replacements were still being sent to Vietnam. Peace negotiations were in progress. Vietnam was winding down, but Americans were still fighting and dying in that war." Public opinion was still savagely against the war. To make matters worse, the discipline and morale of troops in Vietnam had sunk to an all-time low. Drug use had found its way into Southeast Asia, and some wayward conscripts had resorted to "fragging"—murdering officers and NCOs whom they didn't like. As Moore took command of the Army Training Center at Fort Ord, he knew it would take a lot of work to undo the costly damage of the Vietnam era.

"As a result of Nixon's campaign promise, the Pentagon was taking its first steps toward an all-volunteer military." In the 1970s, the Army held Basic Training at six Army Training Centers throughout the US—including Fort Ord, California. In preparation for the end of the draft, Army leaders launched a test program known as Project VOLAR (Volunteer Army). By 1971, Army leaders were aware that the average young recruit was much different than his counterpart twenty years earlier. The social and cultural revolutions of the 1960s had taken their toll on the newer generation. Young recruits (especially teenagers) were more apt to question authority and challenge the existing norms. Likewise, the bad publicity generated by Vietnam turned off many potential recruits. Thus, by changing several aspects of Basic Training, the Army hoped to attract more recruits and improve the retention rates among first-term enlistees.

"The need to improve the image of the Army among the young men it sought to attract," Moore said, "was apparent from the opinion surveys taken by the Army, the Department of Defense, and commercial firms. These surveys revealed that the Army was rated the *lowest* of all the services regarding the opportunity for meaningful work, development of skills, and job satisfaction. They also indicated the Army was thought to have such negative aspects as poor living conditions, make-work, harassment, and curiously enough, the lowest pay, although the pay is the same for all services."

While VOLAR went a long way towards improving the Army's readiness, quality of life, and overall professionalism, several of its concepts were flawed. In fact, VOLAR had compromised many of the Army's long-standing traditions for building good discipline. Grooming standards had been relaxed; Reveille formations had been abolished; marching and close-order drill had been curtailed. Beer was being served in the barracks, and a new "Enlisted Man's Council" allowed soldiers to circumvent the chain of command. VOLAR had even adopted the new recruiting slogan—"Today's Army Wants to Join You"—and barracks were being painted in pastel colors. "The Army, in particular, was getting a lot of bad press on 'Beer in the Barracks,' along with the lowered standards of discipline," Moore said.

Moore realized these permissive attitudes threatened the NCOs role of enforcing discipline and "some [NCOs] became lax in the enforcement of existing rules and regulations." Because Basic Training was supposed to instill discipline and teamwork, Moore decided to change Fort Ord's role in the VOLAR program. "First," he explained, "we put great emphasis on non-commissioned officer authority, responsibility, and performance." It was a nod to one of his earliest leadership lessons—*push the power down*. Because soldiers worked directly for non-commissioned officers, the "responsibilities of Fort Ord's drill sergeants and other NCOs had to be increased." Second, he initiated the same officer and NCO leadership courses he had used in Korea. Under his direction, the Fort Ord Leadership Academy became the nucleus for officer and NCO development. Its purpose was to "improve leadership skills and to develop technical and administrative abilities." Third, he placed a greater emphasis on physical training and mental discipline. "Rigorous physical demands were placed on all," he said, "and we stressed traditional Army discipline such as saluting and precision marching, close order drill, proper wearing of the uniform, and related military customs and courtesies."

The Fort Ord Leadership Academy was critical to ensuring his subordinates' success because, as Moore stated, "the grunts on the front lines, or in the business cubicles, and the middle managers must be continually developed to be good at their jobs. Periodic critiques, required reading, special schooling, and one-on-one mentoring programs are helpful. In any successful activity, you need to have smart people who are motivated and dedicated. In athletics, the teams with the best players almost always win. And so it is in all endeavors. The leader has to keep his people learning, improving their capabilities, and create new imaginative ways to increase their perceptiveness and their efficiency.

"On those occasions when one of my people did not perform as expected, I found that in many cases at least half the fault was my own. I had either not put out clear, clean instructions or I had not trained that person sufficiently, or I had given him a task with little or no possibility of accomplishment."

Reflecting on the need for rigorous discipline, Moore wrote, "The grunts who do the dog work in the trenches are absolutely essential to success. For each to do their duty at their level is just as important and necessary to mission accomplishment as the captains, colonels, and generals are at their level. Even more so. But who are these men? How are they formed? What makes them take on seemingly impossible tasks—fraught with life-ending possibilities? Why? It all begins with what is called 'Basic Training.'"

"These are the demanding weeks of culture and environmental shock, which takes a man or woman from the civilian world into the world of military discipline. This is the time when men of all colors and races drawn from different backgrounds including from farms, cities, ghettos, and small towns are turned into soldiers—not robotic automatons. We blend their distinct personalities with the disciplinary culture—the do's and don'ts of military life. Their separate personalities survive however and often produce the feisty Bill Mauldins (of WWII cartoon fame), and the men who become sergeants and officers." Citing Confucius, Moore then said: "*To lead an untrained people to war is to throw them away.*"

Likewise, Moore knew that Vietnam had changed the nature of warfare. It was the first conflict in modern American history where the frontlines had *disappeared*. In Vietnam, the so-called "rear echelon" had become obsolete. Support personnel—including typists, clerks, cooks, and analysts—now had a greater chance of being engaged by the enemy. These proverbial "clerks and jerks," therefore, needed to have the same level, or nearly the same level, of tactical training as the infantry soldiers.

At the time, Moore wrote: "The business of soldiering has been overtaken by the complexities of the modern world. Today's soldier operates in an environment which requires ever-increasing knowledge of techniques and technology unknown to his forefathers. At the same time, he must possess and develop those basic qualities that have characterized the good soldier through the ages: strength, both mental and physical; discipline, self-confidence and loyalty. The Army continually faces the task of turning citizens into soldiers. The conversion process, Basic Training, has been developed and improved over the years through research, experimentation, and analysis. As the name suggests, the process consists of training all men who enter the Army in the basics of soldiering. A man may enter to become an aviation machinist, a dental technician, or a supply specialist, but he will first learn the basic skills of the infantryman. A case can be made that the teaching of skills which may not subsequently be employed is wasteful in time and money, but experience has proven the need for basic infantry training. First, there can be no guarantee that the aviation machinist or the supply clerk will not someday be obliged to put aside his wrench or stock book in favor of a rifle and bayonet. *American military history is full of such instances, which often occur in guerrilla wars where there is no rear area safe from attack.* Second, the thousands of Army noncombatants that support, supply, and sustain the combat troops, who constitute the cutting edge of the nation's military power, *do their jobs better if they know firsthand the duties of those they support.*

"Basic training is frequently arduous, sometimes onerous, and often dangerous. At the same time, the new soldier is learning to do things, he is learning new attitudes toward people and ideas. The training emphasizes disciplined, confident, individual responsibility but also teaches the importance of group effort. The recruit sees that a team of four can accomplish more than four individuals working separately. Frequently, he must modify the habits and attitudes he brought with him and replace them with group-oriented behavior patterns. The American military tradition has always stressed the need for innovative individuals who see the need for disciplined team effort and self-discipline without which no Army can function effectively."

With these ideas in mind, Moore revised Fort Ord's Basic Training curriculum. In the early days of VOLAR, bayonet training, hand-to-hand combat, obstacle courses, and speed road marches had been abolished. Moore however, re-instituted each of these subjects during his first year of command. "The goal was for every man leaving Basic Combat Training to be in the best physical shape of his life and to know it...to stretch his mind and his muscles and to assist him in thereby gaining more pride in himself, more self-confidence, and above all, more self-discipline." Moore's philosophy was simple:

A man who has more self-discipline has more confidence in his ability to do the job.

"There is a close connection between discipline and confidence. I am not talking about discipline as in remedial measures to rectify improper behavior. Training and discipline are mutually supportive and lead to confidence. Proper training prepares persons for all types of endeavors. Discipline, however, adds to training and natural ability; it develops self-control and team control. Discipline requires dedication and firm commitment.

- Self-discipline (study, self-improvement) leads to self-confidence.
- Disciplined use of technical equipment such as various software programs, charts, records, and comparative study analyses leads to confidence in those tools.
- Organizational discipline and smooth teamwork leads to unit confidence.
- When you put these all together, the result is disciplined, confident

efficiency and professionalism.

Likewise, "men in a unit which has disciplined, competent leaders will have more confidence in those leaders."

Moore also revised the weapons training for his recruits. Up to that point, Basic Training had covered only two weapons: the M16 rifle and the M26 hand grenade—there had been no instruction in heavy infantry weapons, survival tactics, or land mine warfare. Instead, the Army had transferred these topics to Advanced Individual Training (AIT) for Combat Arms soldiers (e.g. infantry, mechanized cavalry scouts, tank crewmen, etc). Moore's approach, added training on the M203 Grenade Launcher, M60 Machine Gun, M72A2 Light Anti-Tank Weapon (bazooka), the Claymore Mine, and introduced survival and evasion tactics to the curriculum. "The transfer of these subjects," he said, "produced both immediate and downstream advantages." After all, in a war like Vietnam, where there were no frontlines and no rear echelons, non-combat soldiers could benefit from learning more than just the standard M-16 rifle.

A good leader trains his people to adapt to changes in the environment or the marketplace.

The complexities of Vietnam demanded a revitalization of the Basic Training system. So, too, in the civilian world, markets and industries evolve. When changes occur, leaders must give their organizations the tools and training to prepare for the new realities. For instance, a multi-billion dollar corporation couldn't survive today if it clung to the technology and business practices of the 1970s. Adapting to changes, and subsequently learning new skill sets, might seem intuitive. However, some organizations are more resistant to change than others. And so it was for the US Army in 1971. Moore spent a considerable time at Fort Ord convincing Army leaders of the need to overhaul VOLAR.

Finally, in the fall of 1971, Moore's training revisions were given a forum at the Modern Volunteer Army Conference at Fort Jackson, South Carolina. "Fort Ord's views," he recalled, "were favorably received and the revised Army training programs published in 1972 made provisions for increased training." This not to say that Moore was solely responsible for the Army's Basic Training overhaul—there were several recommendations made by other Army Training Centers. There can be little argument, however, that Moore's experiments and recommendations had a profound impact on the Basic Training and Advanced Individual Training programs.

In fact, "shifting heavy weapons familiarization and survival tactics to Basic Training allowed the Advanced Individual Training course to use the freed time to expand instruction in the remaining subjects, add new topics, and still stay within the allotted training period."

All the while, Moore was continuously struck by how "the NCOs, in eight weeks' time, could turn those young men of varying diversities, personalities, and backgrounds into soldiers. Each man retained his distinct personality, his uniqueness, his individualism—but all were tempered for the common good. When a young American becomes a soldier, his personality and outlook on life are permanently changed. On arrival at the Training Center, the first person of authority he or she meets is a Drill Sergeant. A non-commissioned officer. The American NCO. The 'Backbone of the Army.' The Army carefully vets Drill Sergeants and trains them for the challenging and important role they play in the basic training system. The job of the training center cadre has always been extremely demanding—the hours are long and the responsibilities are great. It is not unusual for officers and men of the basic combat training battalions and companies to work fourteen hours a day."

At the same time, Moore took great pains to improve the quality of life for everyone at Fort Ord. "The Vietnam War years," he wrote, "saw a strong emphasis on training and the trainee. Perhaps because of the heavy workload and lack of assignment stabilization which characterized this period, there was little evidence of the close-knit camaraderie and friendliness typical of Army posts. To warm the atmosphere and foster community spirit among members of the permanent party [i.e. non-trainees], added emphasis was given to selected proven programs and new projects were started. In 1971, Fort Ord opened a Welcome Center which housed under one roof all possible facilities and services relating to the arrival or departure of people at the Fort Ord complex." Moore's additions also included a registration office for youth activities which included "a variety of year-round sports, recreational, and educational programs designed to appeal to youngsters." Meanwhile, volunteer Army wives staffed the Fort Ord Welcome Center, providing advice and assistance to newly arrived families. "One of their helpful services," Moore remarked, involved lending "useful items such as pots, pans, and playpens to new families who were waiting for household goods to arrive."

To ease the moving process for incoming soldiers and officers, Moore put a sponsor program in effect. "Each man on orders to Fort Ord," he wrote at the time, "has appointed for him a local sponsor of equivalent grade, typically a member of the unit or staff section which the new arrival is slated to join. The sponsor is responsible for writing or telephoning the new man to offer advance information and assistance. Newly arrived wives are given conducted tours by bus during which they visit various agencies on the post."

There was, however, a lingering issue of crime on post. "No other improvements in Army life can be truly effective," said Moore, "if we cannot provide a safe, disciplined environment for soldiers and their families. The era of the Vietnam War had produced by 1970 a post crime rate of considerable proportions." Fort Ord was no exception. To combat the problem, Moore increased the number of military police patrols and established various neighborhood councils. Under these security measures, the crime rate at Fort Ord dropped considerably.

Still, Moore lived in an era of widespread war protests. "Fort Ord," he said, "was the largest and most heavily-populated Army installation in California. As such, it was the prime target for anti-military activities associated with the Vietnam War." Shortly after he took command, actress Jane Fonda (whose traitorous tour of North Vietnam had earned her the nickname "Hanoi Jane") arrived at the gates of Fort Ord with her anti-war group, "Free the Army," or FTA, in tow. "Of course, there would be TV cameras present, and I knew they wanted a photogenic confrontation between soldiers with fixed bayonets…and the flower-power children. I gave instructions that the MPs and civilian gate guards were to stand in front of the gate but there was to be no use of force and no weapons or nightsticks in hand. Not even the most rabid of demonstrators found much joy in the non-confrontation. The TV cameras left and soon, the crowd broke up, furious at our pacifism. Later that day, Ms. Fonda somehow gained entrance and was found in the recreation room of one of my training center barracks talking with new soldiers. My MPs quietly and courteously escorted her off the post.

"On another occasion, I got wind of a large group of protestors who were headed to the other gate of Fort Ord, which was at the city of Seaside, California." Seeking to diffuse the situation before it even started, Moore directed the Provost Marshal to place the oldest, most out-of-shape, civilian gate guard at the entrance. He was ordered just to "stand there silently with his hands folded across his back. No weapon or nightstick on his belt." Arriving at the gate, the protestors were dumbfounded to see a dainty little man who was old enough to be their grandfather. Realizing that they couldn't bring themselves to attack the old man, the crowd quickly dispersed. Little did they know, that just around the corner, a military police platoon had been waiting with fully loaded M–16s, ready to disperse the crowd if things got out of control. "In those years, we dealt with many anti-war protests. It was an interesting time to command an Army post." Yet whenever a group of demonstrators showed up, Moore's guidance was always the same:

Don't overreact. And never overreact to an overreaction.

Any overreaction would play into the hands of the anti-war movement.

When Moore relinquished command of Fort Ord on August 1, 1973, his farewell address reflected on the changing times and the need for continued discipline in the profession of arms (excerpts).

*"We stand here on this field today, in battle uniform with our weapons— from General to Private—not to glorify war or advocate war. We here who have experienced the truth of the battlefield, and the grief and destruction of war at the soldier level know best of its terrible and heartbreaking cost. Rather, we stand here in battle dress to re-state to ourselves and the public who sees us that we are always aware of our mission to be **ready** to respond…to take to the battlefield with discipline and with traditional Army professionalism.*

…

This post has been special because of the exciting work we have been doing to improve Basic and Advanced Training. In this effort, we are always aware and appreciative of the great trainers and effective training of past years. Now, we have taken new training aids and technological advances, and built on the past, to continue to move forward and to improve—always conscious that we must give our soldiers in the ranks the best available training.

*This post is also special to me because of the great professionalism of the non-commissioned officers and senior specialists who are performing here so superbly. My firm conviction is that **the key to discipline is respect for the noncommissioned officer.** Respect by the soldier in the ranks and instant obedience to the orders of the non-commissioned officers—both in garrison and on the battlefield—and further, respect by **commissioned officers** for the authority of the NCOs and the willingness to back them up. Here at this post, we have a great, dedicated team of non-commissioned officers. The troops at the working level **are in their hands.** And they are good hands—always conscious of that traditional hallmark of the US Army: **discipline.** I am forever grateful to Command Sergeant Major Peroddy, who is at my side today, and the great team of non-commissioned officers of this garrison, for whom he has set and maintained top standards of performance.*

…

I very much appreciate and am very grateful for the professional and personal relationships between me and my staff at Fort Ord, and my deputy post commander at the Presidio and at Hunter Liggett, with civic and other officials of the many surrounding communities. I could name many things we have worked on together—but I will say that this extends from seemingly small matters to very important things such as the schooling of our children, to law and order, to the proper, undiscriminating and hospitable treatment of our soldiers.

The understanding and magnificent attitude of government and civic officials and others in all of our working relationships has been outstanding.

For our part, we have done our best to be candid and truthful in our dealings with the public. We have invited thousands of people of all ages from all over California…ranging from children to senior citizens, male and female, on our posts to see what their Army does, to talk with their soldiers, and to eat their soldiers' food in the mess halls. We hope that these policies and actions have improved public understanding and support of their Army. Anyone who is law-abiding and who has a genuine, sincere interest in our activities has always been welcome on this post.

At this time, I bid you all—military friends and civilian friends alike—a warm farewell. Tomorrow, Major General Robert G. Gard will assume command of this installation and I know that this command, under his leadership, will continue to improve its professionalism, quality of Army life, public understanding, and support.

In August 1973, Hal returned to Washington, DC: first as the Commanding General of the Army Personnel Center (1973-74), then as the Deputy Chief of Staff for Personnel (1974-77). In both capacities, he remained at the forefront of rebuilding the post-Vietnam Army. As Deputy Chief of Staff, Moore petitioned Congress to extend enlistment bonuses for combat arms soldiers. Before the House Appropriations Committee in May 1975, Moore testified that although the Army had met its recruiting goals for the fiscal year, it would be harder to meet the same quota next year without extending bonuses for those joining the combat arms (infantry, armor, and artillery). According to Moore, the combat arms community had a harder time attracting and maintaining soldiers "because young men are more interested in learning skills that they can use to earn a living after they leave the Army."

Although his duties as Deputy Chief of Staff mainly kept him confined to DC, Moore still found opportunities to observe field training as the Army rebuilt itself into an all-volunteer force. Ironically, during a visit to Fort Bragg, North Carolina, Moore had a near-death experience aboard a UH-1 helicopter, the same type of mount that carried him through his darkest days in Vietnam.

On July 12, 1976, Moore was at Fort Bragg observing an iteration of the annual ROTC Advanced Camp training. At about 1:35 PM, Moore was leaving the Leadership Reaction Course (a tactical, problem-solving obstacle course) and boarded the helicopter designated to take him and the rest of the observation party to another training site. "I mounted and sat down in the seat in the middle of the helicopter," Moore recalled, "directly to the rear of the two aviators, facing forward. I hooked my seat belt and was not wearing a headset or helmet."

The two pilots started the aircraft without issue but, seconds into the flight, Moore noticed that something was off—"we seemed to take off on a slight leftward flying pattern, rather than flying straight out"—as that was the direction to their intended destination. "At approximately 100 feet altitude, I heard and felt the engine lose power. I heard the main rotor blade begin winding down rapidly." Moore knew that the aircraft was in trouble.

Maintaining his composure, however, Moore quickly scanned to his left and right, searching for any open areas on the ground that might help the inevitable crash landing.

"I saw none."

At that time, he realized that "the only choice for the pilots was to land in the woods as carefully and softly as possible. There was very little time for reaction. We headed for the ground very rapidly."

"I braced my feet against the back of the pilot's seat. The helicopter hit the ground very hard." Indeed, Moore was surprised at the force of impact. Shaken, stunned, and with a sharp pain across his lower back, Moore was lucky at least to have retained consciousness. Fearful that the helicopter would explode or catch fire, Moore shouted: "Everybody get out of here!" As he attempted to open the helicopter door, however, he noticed that the cadet who had been selected to accompany them on the ride had been injured. To make matters worse, she couldn't unfasten her seat belt. "I dismounted, went to her location and, standing on the ground, I also noticed that the rotor blade was slightly moving." Moore assisted the young cadet by unfastening her seat belt and lifted her out of the wreckage. "Holding her arm, I ran her ahead of me, stumbling, into the trees to the right of the helicopter. "She was evacuated to the hospital with the others for a medical check."

Moore circled the wreckage, looking for anyone who may have needed medical attention. "I noted at that time two or three individuals lying on the ground on the left side of the helicopter, 5-10 meters from it. They were not motionless, but were obviously in pain. I yelled out to everyone to stay away from the helicopter because of possible fire or explosion. I asked if the switches were off, and two or three individuals (I can't remember who) yelled back and said the fuel and battery switches were off. By then, some soldiers appeared with litters and began placing the injured on the litters. I was also informed the medevac helicopter and ground ambulances were on the way. I then briefly checked the two or three individuals who seemed to be more severely injured than the others and confirmed they were getting attention from the personnel associated with the Leadership Reaction Course training site. I cautioned loudly to everybody in the area to stay away from the helicopter and not to go near it. After several minutes, the medevac helicopter and the ground ambulance arrived, and the injured were being taken care of by the medics."

Taking time to assess his own injuries, Moore noted his back, chest, and stomach were in pain but attributed it to nothing more than the shock of impact. "I also had slight cuts on my face and mouth." Once the injured had been tended to and the crash site secured, Hal continued with his scheduled itinerary. After leaving the next training site, he headed over to Fort Bragg's Emergency Clinic where he visited the injured parties and had his own health evaluated. While awaiting his own medical treatment, Moore had a chance to speak with one of the pilots of the ill-fated helicopter. "I thought that he and the other aviator had done extremely well with what they had to work with…he had flared the helicopter as much as he could." The Army later confirmed the mechanical error was not the fault of the pilots'.

"I was then checked out and, after X-Rays and other tests, was told I had a compressed fracture of the L-1 vertebra and a broken rib on the left side in addition to a cracked suborbital bone under my right eye. The hospital commander offered to admit me to the hospital; however, I felt that I could return back to Washington on the U-21 which brought me down, and get medical treatment in DC." Although Moore recovered from the crash, and was given a clean bill of health, he was plagued by back problems for the remainder of his life. Later, when discussing the accident, he concluded he should not have braced his legs against the seat in front as that transferred the force of the impact into his back.

During his time as Deputy Chief of Staff, Moore worked directly for the Army Chief of Staff, General Bernard Rogers. A 1943 West Point graduate, Rogers had been the top-ranking cadet in his class before commissioning as an Infantry Officer. Although he missed combat in World War II, he later served in Korea from 1952-53 and eventually deployed to Vietnam as the assistant commander of the 1st Infantry Division. In 1969, Rogers took command of the 5th Infantry Division, then stationed at Fort Carson, Colorado. At the time, the division "was considered to be one of the most disorganized and unprepared units in the Army"—a reputation that would plague the unit well into the 1990s. "Racial conflict and drug abuse were serious problems"—just as they had been for Moore's outfit in Korea. Despite their similar backgrounds and experience in dealing with drug-addled, race-baiting soldiers, Moore's and Rogers' leadership styles were remarkably different. Rogers was known to be confrontational with an "in-your-face" attitude and wouldn't think twice about publicly berating a subordinate. His style was the polar opposite of Moore's.

Still, Moore had no qualms about taking Rogers to task on policies that would hurt the Army. According to Joe Galloway, "Moore opposed the top brass when they ordered him to dilute recruiting standards to 'make the numbers.'" To Hal Moore, these lower recruiting standards had produced many of the same problems the Army had seen in Vietnam. Lowering the standards to meet personnel quotas would not improve the Army's professional image. Instead, he argued recruiting bonuses had to continue; the "zero-tolerance" drug policy had to remain in effect, and the Army had to keep pushing its public relations campaign to convince potential recruits that military service was a marketable skill. "And," Galloway added, "he argued vehemently when they ordered him to begin assigning women to support jobs with the 82nd Airborne Division's Ready Brigade. Moore said since women could not deploy to combat in those days, the Ready Brigade would have to leave thirty percent of its support troops at home when they left on a 12-hour notice. Jimmy Carter's Secretary of the Army, Clifford Alexander, came down on Hal."

In the heat of this bureaucratic showdown, however, General Rogers tapped Moore to become the Commanding General, US Army Japan. The assignment might have led to a fourth star—the pinnacle rank for a peacetime General. To an outsider, this may have seemed like a promising endeavor. But Moore realized it was a ruse—US Army Japan was a "paper Corps" consisting of "forty clerks and eighty filing cabinets." In effect, the Army's top brass was dangling the four-star rank in front of Moore, hoping to send him to the Pacific where he could no longer disrupt their chorus of "yes men." Having fulfilled most of his goals as an Army officer and refusing to play along with the Beltway bureaucracy, Moore politely turned down the opportunity and retired on August 1, 1977. His culminating lesson was this:

Stand up for principles; choose the "harder right" over the "easier wrong."

Completing thirty-two years of service, Moore concluded that his *personal* reasons for retiring were just as valid as his *professional* reasons. The new assignment in Japan "would have required leaving our children once again at a critical time. Julie's mother was in bad health. I turned it down and in the military, when one turns down a promotion, resignation follows." Before this, there had been muffled talk that Moore was poised to be the next Chief of Staff of the Army—or even Chairman of the Joint Chiefs. But, "my decision was made and I have not regretted the decision and never looked back once." As Joe Galloway succinctly recalled: "He left DC swearing he would never set foot in the Pentagon again and would never become a Beltway Bandit—hitting up old comrades for defense contracts. And he never did."

On the eve of Moore's retirement, his friend and fellow officer, Lieutenant General Henry Emerson, wrote to him: "I respect you more than any officer currently on active duty. To me, it's shameful that you are not either the Chief of Staff of the 8th Army Commander. I just don't know where the Army will turn for a real fighter after you retire."

SUMMARY

A leader should never tell an outfit that it's screwed up. If he does, then it will be screwed up. Why? Because the boss said so.

If you seek to correct a subordinate's overall behavior or performance, start by telling them what they do well, then tell them where they need to improve.

A man who has more self-discipline has more confidence in his ability to do the job.

A good leader trains his people to adapt to changes in the environment or the marketplace.

Don't overreact. And don't overreact to an overreaction.

Stand up for principles; choose the "harder right" over the "easier wrong."

STACKING UP: MOORE'S OFFICER EVALUATION REPORTS

A n officer's performance record is documented on their Officer Evaluation Reports (OERs). Upon completion of any assignment—whether a platoon leader, company commander, or tactical instructor—the officer receives an OER written by their immediate supervisor and endorsed by the next-higher echelon command. Accordingly, a platoon leader (lieutenant) would receive an OER written by his company commander (typically a captain) and endorsed by the battalion commander (lieutenant colonel). Every officer strives to have a well-written OER that contains the right mix of buzzwords that will resonate with the promotion board.

Hal Moore's evaluations reflect his growth and development as a leader. From his earliest assignments, it was clear that he had an infectious enthusiasm and a brand creativity that inspired his subordinates and superiors alike. That is not to say, however, that Moore was "perfect"—like anyone else, he had his shortcomings, setbacks, and the occasional lapse in good judgment. In fact, he wasn't always rated highly by his bosses. Yet at every turn, he (a) took the opportunity to learn from his mistakes and (b) served under leaders who were willing to mentor him.

Moore's first OER—dated December 1945—comes from 1LT Edmund Donnelly, his first company commander in the 187th Glider Regiment. He writes that Moore is a "competent, enthusiastic, and energetic leader. He is well-liked by the men, commanding their respect, and increases their interest in their work."

Of particular note is Donnelly's use of the words "commands their respect"—not "demands their respect." In the context of organizational leadership, *commanding* and *demanding* carry different connotations. Commanding respect is inspired by ones *actions*—treating others with dignity and respect; and giving clear, unambiguous guidance. Demanding respect is simply making a verbal demand and coercing compliance through one's positional authority. Often, this attitude will produce an organization that either (a) fails, or (b) perennially meets the minimum standard because no one is inspired to excel.

Moore continued his trend of positive leadership throughout his service in Occupied Japan. His next few OERs—covering his service as the Camp Construction Officer—rate him as "Superior" in every dimension. However, by the Spring of 1947, Moore's superiors rated him a 4 out of 7 for "Judgment and Common Sense" and a 5 out of 7 for the dimensions of "Attention to Duty," "Force," and "Ability." Qualitatively, this still placed Moore in the "Excellent" rating category (see Figure 1) but it was his lowest rating during the time when the Army used this system of evaluation. This lower rating was likely due to the river rafting incident in Hokkaido that cost the life of a fellow lieutenant (which would have occurred at around this time). The most glaring critique of Moore on this OER was that he was "inclined to be slightly over-severe in his requirements of the men who have not yet reached the state of training expected"—although it's not clear what the evaluator meant by this. It may have been a reference to the punitive runs or that Moore simply needed to dial back his expectations for the newly-arriving soldiers.

One of Moore's final OERs from his duty in Occupied Japan comes from Major Herbert Mansfield, whom Moore described as a great leader and a significant influence on his life as a young officer. From the tone of Mansfield's narrative, it is evident he saw and appreciated Moore's potential. He also took the time to *mentor* Moore and point out areas for improvement while still accentuating the positive. This is mentoring at its core. In any large organization there is a tendency to minimize and neglect mentoring and move to "zero defects," metrics-based leadership approach because it's easier. Too often, enthusiastic contributors are cut down by leaders who don't take the time to mentor them or help them refine their skills. These leaders forget that their subordinates need mentoring and guidance to learn and grow into assets to the organization. Instead, in that negative framework, any honest mistake, breach of organizational etiquette, or misguided initiative results in a reprimand and an associated "black mark" against the subordinate.

EFFICIENCY REPORT
See AR 600–185 for details.

Unit Adjutant or Personnel Officer will complete Sections I and III.
Rating Officer will complete Sections IV, V, VI, VII, VIII, and IX.
Indorsing Officer will complete Sections II, V, VII, and IX.

INFANTRY

Section I. OFFICER REPORTED UPON

Use typewriter or print in ink. Use carbon paper to fill out Section III at same time. See AR 600–185.

B4

DO NOT WRITE IN THIS SPACE

FIRST NAME	INITIAL	SERIAL NUMBER	GRADE	ARM OR SERVICE	COMPONENT	PERIOD OF REPORT FROM	TO
HAROLD	G., JR.	027 678	1st Lt	Infantry	RA	7Jul47	29Feb48

UNIT, ORGANIZATION AND STATION	PRIMARY MOS	DUTY ASSIGNMENT (MOS CODE)	DAYS OF DUTY	LEAVE	OTHER NON-DUTY
Hq&Hq Co,187th Gli Inf 11th Abn Div, APO 468	1512	2162	238	None	None

FOR REPORTS RENDERED BECAUSE OF PERMANENT CHANGE OF STATION, SUPPLY ADDRESS OF UNIT AND INSTALLATION WHERE OFFICER WILL REPORT
Semiannual report, paragraph 6c(4), AR 600-185

GRADE, AND ORGANIZATION OR UNIT OF RATING OFFICER
T V. MANSFIELD, Maj, O 361 345
Glider Infantry

NAME, GRADE, AND ORGANIZATION OR UNIT OF INDORSING OFFICER
GEORGE O. PEARSON, Lt Col, 039 592
187th Glider Infantry

Section II. DATA AND SUGGESTIONS FOR USE IN ASSIGNMENT

NOTE: Information on this page will be forwarded to the Career Branch of the Personnel and Administration Division by TAG after ratings have been determined. Proper future assignment and utilization of the officer will depend upon the care with which information in this section is formulated and reported. Use typewriter or print in ink.

DUTIES ACTUALLY PERFORMED ON PRESENT JOB. To be supplied by Rater. Be specific. Give his duty assignment and all additional duties with enough specific detail to show scope of job in each area. Liaison Officer, Regimental S-3 Section. Principally concerned with air ground liaison, planning and execution of parachute operations; construction and planning of tactical maneuver problems.

DESCRIPTION OF OFFICER RATED AND COMMENTS. These paragraphs should cover physical, mental, moral qualities of rated officer, specialties of value to the Army, and any special defects or weaknesses affecting his ability to do certain assignments.

COMMENTS OF RATING OFFICER Rugged young officer whose physic appearance and aptitudes preeminently fit for parachute command. Clean-lived, willing worker. Has exceptional ability as anti-jumper. I have brought to the attention of this officer any weaknesses indicated herein.

COMMENTS OF INDORSING OFFICER I concur and add: This officer will tackle anything. Sometimes carried away by his own enthusiasm but sincere and honest in his intentions and motifs. Possesses a casualness socially that is sometimes mistaken for rudeness. I have brought to the attention of this officer any weaknesses indicated herein.

ESTIMATED DESIRABILITY IN VARIOUS CAPACITIES. Assume you are a commander of a major unit in war. Indicate to what extent you would want the rated officer to serve under you in the next higher grade in the type of duty described below. Place an X in the proper box, using the h and NA area if the duty is not applicable. If line h is used, specify the nature of specialty.

	RATER NA	1	2	3	4	5	INDORSER NA	1	2	3	4	5
Represent your viewpoint and make decisions in your name at a higher headquarters.					X						X	
Command a unit immediately subordinate to you on a combat mission.						X						X
Responsible in an emergency calling for initiative, coolness, forceful leadership.						X						X
On an assignment requiring great attention to detail and routine.					X						X	
In all aspects of a military situation, using judgment, initiative, and coolness.						X						X
Represent you where tact and ability to get along with people are needed.						X					X	
On an assignment as specialist or technician. (Specify.)	X						X					
Carry out the duties of the type of work to which he is now assigned.						X						X

IMMEDIATE RECOMMENDATIONS FOR CAREER DEVELOPMENT. Be specific.

RATER'S RECOMMENDATION FOR ASSIGNMENT (MOS CODE)
Parachute Infantry Unit Commander (1510)

INDORSER'S RECOMMENDATION FOR ASSIGNMENT (MOS CODE)
Parachute Infantry Unit Commander (1510)

RATER'S RECOMMENDATION FOR FURTHER TRAINING
Advance at Branch School

INDORSER'S RECOMMENDATION FOR FURTHER TRAINING
Advanced Course
The Infantry School

RATINGS ARE BASED ON → (RATER WILL CHECK)	INTIMATE DAILY CONTACT	FREQUENT OBSERVATION OF THE RESULTS OF HIS WORK	INFREQUENT OBSERVATION OF THE RESULTS OF HIS WORK	ACADEMIC RECORDS	OFFICIAL REPORTS
	X				

WAGO FORM

IBM FORM I.T.S. 1100 F

Figure 1. Hal Moore's OER from the Spring of 1948. Written by Major Herbert Mansfield, it accentuates the positive while indicating Moore's potential for advancement and continued promotion. *The Harold G. Moore Collection*

Mansfield writes: "This officer will tackle anything. Sometimes carried away by his own enthusiasm but sincere and honest in his intentions and motifs. Possesses a casualness socially that is sometimes mistaken for rudeness. I have brought to the attention of this officer any weaknesses indicated herein." Still, Mansfield rated him highly across all leadership dimensions and recommended him for further advancement.

When Moore deployed to Korea, his OERs reflect an officer coming into his own. While settling into his new job as the Regimental S-3, his superiors described him as a "bright, enthusiastic officer. He sees that a job is completed and sets an example to the command by his attitude. He achieves superior results." These observations are reflected further in two additional OERs from his service at the division-level echelons in Korea. Sadly, the OERs from his command of the mortar company have not survived.

As a tactics instructor at West Point, we see Moore's superiors recognizing one of his most fundamental leadership traits in action—loyalty going up *and* down the chain of command. They write that: "His subordinates are required to produce results and maintain high discipline, which they do, assisted by the personal example set by Major Moore. His primary job of military instruction has been accomplished with much initiative and infectious enthusiasm. *Loyalty is exerted in both directions* [emphasis added]."

Perhaps his most glowing recommendations came in the wake of his leadership in the Ia Drang Valley. After establishing himself as a battalion commander without equal during the days of the 11th Air Assault Division, his superiors were not surprised by his remarkable leadership in Vietnam. General Harry WO Kinnard writes [with emphasis added throughout]: "I have had the privilege of serving with this peerless officer for almost three years, during which he commanded a matchless battalion until 29 Nov 65. Then, following his promotion, he took command of the 3d Brigade, 1st Cavalry Division (Airmobile). He is being rated in this report as a brigade commander in combat. As such, he has continued to exhibit remarkable traits of leadership which mark him as one of the Army's very top combat commanders of his grade. He assumed his higher responsibilities quickly and easily and molded a responsive, deadly fighting command that has exacted a terrible toll from the enemy. *He has unusual tactical intuition and judgment found in only a very few officers.* He seems to be able to "smell" the enemy and plans and operates in such a way as to repeatedly outsmart and outfight him. He is personally bold in battle, almost, I repeat, almost to a fault. He goes where the fighting is hardest and there makes his own on-the-ground assessment of what to do. *His subordinates love him and would follow him anywhere.*

"He is, at the same time an efficient administrator and a thorough, sound planner. He is very articulate and has a unique ability to describe combat situations. Moore is one of our topmost fighting colonels who is daily adding to the luster of his already deservedly bright reputation. I have recommended him for the DSC and his unit (with others) for the Presidential Unit Citation. He is a brand new colonel but is already a clear cut candidate for promotion to brigadier general as soon as he is in the zone for consideration. I would be delighted to serve with him again. *I wish the Army had more Hal Moores."*

At the conclusion of his service in Vietnam, Moore's superiors continued reporting his peerless leadership. In his OER dated November 1, 1966, they write: "Colonel Moore's performance was thoroughly outstanding in all respects. A very seasoned combat leader, he consistently produced overwhelming victories against determined North Vietnamese and Viet Cong forces of reinforced battalion size. In two major operations, DAVY CROCKETT and NATHAN HALE each of about two weeks duration, he fought his brigade (two to five battalions of infantry with supporting arms) under a wide variety of combat conditions with remarkable success. *His leadership was brilliant, resourceful, forceful, colorful and highly inspiring.* He possesses a consummate knowledge of tactics and weapons which he has skillfully adapted to combat conditions in Vietnam. *He has mastered far better than most the problems of fighting the VC and this environment.* He runs a smooth, trim operation off the battlefield and achieves a very high order of discipline when the pressures of combat have been removed. His demonstrated ability to express himself, both orally and in writing, is an outstanding characteristic which makes him stand out among his contemporaries. *Colonel Moore has been awarded the DSC and recommended for the DSM for his outstanding service in Vietnam and for pioneering the Army's new doctrine of air mobility.* He has fully deserved this distinction. He should be promoted to general officer at the earliest practicable time and ahead of his contemporaries.

"The performance of this officer in combat has been so much above that of other commanders of high caliber as to be in a class by himself. I would entrust command of a division to him today."

That command came on the tail of a massive race riot in the 7th Infantry Division. After curtailing the 7th Division's racial and disciplinary problems, here is what Moore's superiors had to say: "General Moore has done a superbly outstanding job as Commanding General of the 7th Infantry Division. Possessed by a keen sense of dedication, unflagging energy and highly motivated, he has done all jobs assigned to him in an exemplary manner. *He analyzed a difficult race relations situation and solved it with firmness and tact.* He showed uncommon initiative and exhibited great professional leadership in installing high standards of training, maintenance and discipline within his division. He commanded the unit during the difficult drawdown period and turned in his equipment in far better shape than he found it. He took great pains to develop his juniors and led them not only by teaching, but by personal example."

Meanwhile, General Michaelis, who had hand-picked Moore for command of the Division, added his endorsement: "MG Moore has demonstrated, under extremely difficult conditions, those attributes of personal decorum, highest professional standards, and superb leadership, which led to enthusiastic loyalty from his subordinates and complete confidence of his seniors. I consider this young General Officer to be an outstanding Division Commander who led by example and accepted only the highest duty standards from himself and his subordinates. *Of particular importance, in this day of dissent, was General Moore's ability to communicate with his personnel—to be familiar and conversant with their problems, imagined or actual.* The outstanding capabilities of General Moore are exemplified by his handling of minority problems; the confidence placed in General Moore by minorities; and the confidence of all other races and creeds in their commander."

After one year in command at Fort Ord, Moore's OER highlighted the importance of empathy and interpersonal tact. "Ingenious, aggressive, keenly intelligent and discerning, MG Moore is a top-flight leader who has wrought innumerable improvements in the command and management of Fort Ord. *Possessed of an unusual empathy with people in general and troops in particular, his leadership during a period of social tumult has been nothing short of inspired.* He is a soldier-oriented General who has proven himself a total advocate and practitioner of equal opportunities for all. General Moore's superbly outstanding performance was characterized by a very imaginative and innovative approach to the challenge of training young men for today's Army without prejudicing military discipline."

His last available OER comes from his tenure as the commander of the Army's Military Personnel Center (MILPERCEN) in 1974. It lists his accomplishments in helping reform the Army's personnel system in the wake of the Vietnam War. Written by Army Chief of Staff General Bernard Rogers (ironically the same man who would clash with Moore a few years later), it reads: "He leads a dynamic, resourceful and innovative organization and leads it well. His influence is being felt throughout the Army's personnel system. His involvement in the implementation of the Officer Personnel Management System, the development of the Enlisted

Personnel Management System, the development of a new Officers Efficiency Report [before it was renamed the Officer Evaluation Report], and in other areas will have a long-term impact upon the Army. He should be promoted to lieutenant general." Within months of this OER being published, Moore received that promotion and was accelerated to his ultimate position as Deputy Chief of Staff for Personnel.

APPENDIX A:
LIEUTENANT LEADERSHIP IN COMBAT

By Harold G. Moore, Colonel, Infantry

(Note: Hal Moore wrote this monograph a few months after returning from Vietnam. While oriented specifically to a military audience, there is a direct translation for civilian readers. Think of a Lieutenant as a junior supervisor who leads several small teams, each of which has a team leader (aka NCO). The same obligations exist in both military and civilian environments to lead, motivate and take care of the troops/employees. Finally, in the civilian context, the mention of weapon translates to tools; fighting = working, etc.)

This is a compilation of a few of my views on the leadership of and by Lieutenants. Specifically, infantry platoon leaders in a combat zone. It will be somewhat mixed in perspective, and it is not possible in these few words to get across my full views on leadership. In my judgment, a leader builds, over time, his own unique brand of empathy (or lack of it) with his subordinates and creates his own leadership debits and credits with those under his orders. He does this through personal contact and shared experiences based on the interplay between leader and led, working with mixed perspectives shaped by the dynamics of real time and real life.

Leadership is a highly personal, individual matter. Each leader must establish his own approach based on an internal compass using a method geared to his personality, his capabilities but always oriented towards accomplishing the mission while knowing and taking care of his men.

As officers, we are given groups of men to lead; other officers, NCOs, and enlisted soldiers. Each has a different background, different problems, a different outlook and different duties. But, no matter what their background or their previous experience, no matter now much love, care, and effort may have been spent over the years by their parents in raising them when they are turned over to us all are now ours to care for. At that instant, the parents, teachers or system that brought them to that point will be in the past. Their lives and their future are largely in our hands. This is a terrible responsibility for a Fire Team leader to have - not to speak of a Battalion, a Division or a Corps Commander.

At the Platoon Leader's level, this is brought home with tremendous impact because there are so few men in a platoon. He gets to know each intimately and, if he does his job, becomes exceptionally familiar with the personal, mental environment within which each man performs his duty. This is essential. Those mental situations can range from the mature outlook of the beautifully professional but possibly financially strapped NCO with four kids to the homesick, 19-year-old, inattentive Private away from home, parents, and girlfriend for the first time who worries about being cut out of the pattern by some guy with a draft deferment. To repeat, the point I am making is the men are completely in our hands when we have command jobs. We must take care them and look out for their welfare.

Now, this not only means seeing the troops are fed, clothed and housed properly (the easy part), but more importantly, training them to perfection, anticipating their problems and needs while actively anticipating and eliminating problems before they occur. Among other attributes, I feel soldiers of any rank must have confidence in four directions.

The first is to have self-confidence. Developing it leverages many sources. The primary source is expert knowledge of his assigned duties and readiness, at any time, to take on the next higher job. In addition to creating confidence through individual expertise, his superiors facilitate its development through trust and how they treat him. This is imperative. Every person's dignity must always be respected. I feel that if anyone under me fails, the fault is at least half mine. A man should never be caused to think poorly of himself, and this requires a subtle and sensitive touch by the leader; especially when taking disciplinary action.

Second, but not in priority order, is the necessity for each to have complete confidence in his personal weapon as well as any other weapon he might have to handle to include using radios and the knowing the procedures for requesting and controlling mortar and artillery fires. Developing this takes leader-controlled, leader-supervised training.

Third, confidence in the unit and the men who are fighting with him. At whatever level, the leader must strive to develop an intense esprit de corps. But never by running down other units. An example of what not to do is to permit internal sub-units to be so disloyal to the organization as a whole as to criticize, snipe or run down sister units - be it a squad, platoon, or company on up. It is self-defeating and tears down the unit as a whole

Fourth, and so vital, a man must have confidence and trust in his leaders. He must know and utterly believe his leaders are competent professionals who know what they are doing and are not careless or casual in their outlook toward their responsibilities. For a subordinate to be confident in his leader, the subordinate must know the leader is aware of and appreciates what the subordinate must face and the life he must lead in performing his job. The leader must make every effort to get inside the heads of his men and see their problems and the world from their viewpoint. This takes some doing, and while the leader cannot be intrusive into personal affairs, he must help solve personal problems – if he can – especially if the problems penalize individual or unit performance. For example, in garrison, and to some extent even in a combat area, most disciplinary problems stem from women, alcohol, firearms control, money, and vehicles. Knowing this, a leader can perform a lot of preventive maintenance. As an isolated, but not a sole example, pay problems often arise for separated families living on a limited income. Many of these can be eliminated in advance by real leadership.

In summary, my views are: take care of the troops, develop four-way confidence and be professional. This ensures we can carry out our first duty – accomplishment of the mission. Finally, concerning professionalism, I believe even now the clock is bringing us closer to some few seconds, minutes or hours in the future when the professionalism we will have, or will not have, will make a life or death difference for the men placed under our leadership and whose families can only trust, hope, and pray we know our business.

APPENDIX B:
"WE SHALL PREVAIL"

Speech given at the National Press Club in Washington, DC – September 17, 2007

I imagine there are few here today as old as I—85 years. I cannot help but reflect on my having been just around the corner here in Washington, DC, in early 1940. I was 18 years old and in a strange city. But I had a dream.

From age 15, my goal, my dream was to get into the US Military Academy at West Point and become an Army Officer, but I was unable to get an appointment. Then, the local representative of US Senator Happy Chandler was told that the Senate had an opening in the US Senate Book Warehouse under his patronage. I was offered the job and I grabbed it. I figured I would have a far better chance of finding an appointment to West Point on the ground in Washington than writing letters in the middle of Kentucky. I left Bardstown, Kentucky, two days later for Washington and the warehouse job. In retrospect, that decision was the major turning point in my life.

I continued the pursuit of my dream for two years.

I asked my Congressman for his West Point appointment but he had already given it to another boy; however, at my request he gave me his Annapolis Naval Academy appointment. I then asked if he would agree to a swap if I could pull it off. He agreed, and ten days later I had an appointment to West Point from Georgia Congressman Eugene F. Cox. I graduated in 1945, and became a 2d Lieutenant Infantry paratrooper.

I had prevailed.

In November 1965, in Vietnam, my 450 men of the 1st Battalion, 7th

Cavalry and I leaped out of Huey helicopters in Vietnam into a valley of death—the Ia Drang Valley. We were quickly surrounded by an estimated 2,000 North Vietnamese enemy determined to kill all of us; we were in deep trouble. After three days and nights of fierce fighting, the surviving enemy withdrew into Cambodian sanctuary after losing more than 1,000 killed. We lost 79. The battle was over.

Not once during that non-stop shoot-out did it cross my mind that we might go down. I believed that we would prevail. And we did. But we paid the price.

I share this experience with you because to believe that you will prevail, in any endeavor, means everything.

Our country has faced major crises. The Civil War, the 1929 financial crisis and the early 30s Depression, Pearl Harbor, the Cuban Missile Crisis, the Civil Rights era, 9/11, and financial problems. With each crisis, there always seems to be a combination of factors that enables America to eventually prevail.

Not every crisis is one where blood spills forth. In many cases, a burgeoning national crisis is one in which its people are gravely troubled within; where slow moving negative forces can become a national plague; wherein a nation cries from within. And yet, with the naked eye, we often do not pay sufficient attention to this kind of situation.

I believe that America is crying from within now—in a different kind of crisis.

Today, September 17, 2007, I speak of a national negative condition, a new kind of insidious enemy that is striking at the public's confidence in our national institutions. In the June 21, 2007 Gallup News Service update on America's Confidence in Institutions Survey three weeks ago, I quote:

"Gallup's annual update on American's confidence in institutions shows that confidence ratings are generally down across the board compared to last year. The public's confidence ratings in several institutions, including Congress, are now at an all-time low. Of the 16 societal institutions tested in Gallup's 2007 update, Americans express the most confidence in the military."

Early in my 32 years of active duty, including battlefield infantry combat for over two years in two major wars in the Far East, I learned that trust is the mandatory ingredient in a military unit of any size, and that it has to work in three directions:

- The leader must have trust in the people he leads; trust that they will perform their duties well.

- The people in the ranks must have trust in their leaders; trust that they will perform their duties completely.

- The people in the ranks must have trust and confidence in one another; trust that each will perform their duties well as members of the team.

If any one of these three elements of trust is missing, that military unit cannot be trusted to succeed in its mission. I believe that these three directions of trust can be applied to all organizations, including governmental. Excellence in government cannot be reached without public trust.

The condition, as clearly shown in the 2007 Gallup Poll, is that in many institutions, public trust is at an all-time low. But this national malaise can be changed. America has always prevailed against the enemy. And we will prevail again and again. In our greatest of crises, we have prevailed. And we will prevail now—but for a different cause—with a re-awakening of public trust.

I stand before you representing many who believe in America. I remind you of the fierce urgency of showing up, standing up, and speaking up for the importance of public trust in our nation.

We all have to start somewhere. May today be the beginning of something very good, may today be the beginning of better government in America, for America. In this, we must prevail. Make no mistake about it. Americans believe that we can turn the worst into the best of outcomes, and we usually do.

We must all live and trust in the larger sense. Not to do so will eventually spell the end of what our Constitution so boldly achieves—that we trust in each other and our nation. This most important document has brought "unrest to rest, disorder to order, and failures and faults to perfection." It has done so since 1776 and it can do so again.

At all times, our Constitution has been the bedrock of public trust and the foundation for all of us to believe that America is worthy of all that we can give—to include our lives if and when necessary. Because of it, we can be more deliberate in everything with the deliberation that will characterize every nation. Our Constitution has allowed us and has instructed us not to act in haste, when all indicators would have suggested so.

Why have we, and why will we prevail once more? *Because of our Constitution*. But there are also other reasons why we will prevail in advancing public trust in America.

Americans live with a positive attitude. Make no mistake about it. Americans believe that we can turn the worst into the best of outcomes, and we usually do. Our history says so. Not only do we have a positive attitude, we are a people of action, commitment and perseverance. Action is an American way of life.

Equal to our nation's attitude and sense of action, is our leadership. When we seem to be in crises of the worst kind, there are leaders, or a leader, in America who have stepped up and led us through the worst into a better way of life, thus increasing public trust.

What is there about our great nation that does not accept defeat? What is it about our great nation that does not allow self-interests to override the interests of all?

I believe the answer lies in trusting on another.

Some of you may question the subject matter of public trust and not see it as a threat to our nation. "No blood, no crisis." I see it another way: "No trust = a grave threat to our nation."

Americans have always come together as one, to tackle a problem as one. We have never flinched when we knew what was right! Many of you know that today, the 17th of September, is the day in 1787 that the Constitution was drafted. This started public trust in America.

This is our goal: increasing public trust.

It will require much time and intermediate objectives, but I am convinced that each achievement of an intermediate objective will stack the deck for increasing public trust. Incrementally, we shall prevail. The time is now. America is full of great examples of how one person changed a negative situation or improved a situation. I challenge each of you to think about your family, workplace, and how you might help to advance public trust in your environment. If you do not, who will?

I believe we shall prevail…once again. As written in our currency, "In God we trust."

"WITHOUT EQUAL: WE!"

*Speech delivered to Anheuser-Busch distributors at the
Arie Crown Theater in Chicago — April 10, 2008*

I suppose we all have certain personal "bumper stickers" that remain with us throughout life. One such "bumper sticker" with me is:

> *There is always one more thing you can do to influence a situation in your favor. And after that, one more thing.*

I wish to reference this during my days on the battlefield, and in life. On November 14, 1965, three o' clock in the afternoon, Lt. Col. Nguyen Huu An of the North Vietnamese Army and I were trying our best to kill each other in the Ia Drang Valley of South Vietnam, by the Cambodian Border.

I was a 43-year-old Lt. Col, commanding a 450-man infantry battalion in the first major battle of the Vietnam War. We were up against over 2,000 North Vietnamese regulars. *I believe that three principles of leadership, and our will to win, guided us during the 54-hour shootout. First: never quit. Second: attitude. Third: trust your instincts.*

On the third day, November 16, 1965, the enemy quit the fight leaving over 600 dead and weapons littering the field. We lost 79 of my precious men killed, 121 wounded, none missing. We were a well-trained, tightly-disciplined family team of fighting warriors.

As I walked the bloody and scarred battlefield, I knew that it was, without question, our will to win that made the difference between life or death for my battalion.

In any endeavor, there is always one more thing you can do to influence the situation in your favor. With regard to this battle, near the end of it, the one thing I could and did do, was to charge the enemy when things were spotty. That bayonet charge stunned the enemy: we took it to them I when believe they thought we were on our heels.

As I visit with you today, some 42 years plus later, I can still smell the blood stained soil, hear bullets whizzing by, hear the cries of men going down, and see the land that war had changed forever. And I can see the faces of my men, men I carried to the helicopters, dying in my arms.

Our will to win could not be denied. We would prevail at all costs—and we did prevail, but not without the greatest of human sacrifice and the terrible impact death has on families back home.

Seventeen months earlier, back at Fort Benning, Georgia, on the very first day I took command, I stood in front of my officers and men and told them:

"We're a good battalion, but we're gonna get a hell of a lot better. I will do my best and expect the same from each of you. We will be…without equal. We will be the best infantry battalion in the world! Now go back to your barracks and get rid of all 2nd place trophies. From now on, only 1 st place trophies will be awarded, accepted, or displayed in this outfit. In our line of work, if we come in second, we are defeated on the battlefield. From now on, we are interested only in winning! We are without equal!"

For us then, and in many other battles, the will to win was the only acceptable mindset. This required the creation of an institutional culture of skilled, smooth teamwork; an institutional personality of a warming outfit; and for every warrior to believe and act like he was a winner. For a positive, upbeat institutional culture—institutional persona—was critical to our, and your, success.

I say to you, "You are without equal!" To be without equal means to prevail. To win. It is here where I believe that we should discuss where the will to win comes from, in every person who laces up his or her boots, or who puts on your coat of honor. But before we do, I wish to propose a thought to you:

WITHOUT EQUAL. Think about it.

These words are even more powerful than the "Will to Win" or "#1"… ponder the feeling one gets from these words. I suggest you, embrace these words forever within your institution. And as you enlarge your circles around the world, make these two words your everyday life breath.

Look at what the words start with W and E—meaning "WE." If the

Army approved and supplied the pins, and you were my battalion and we were going to war, I would have every soldier wear a pin with the letters "WE," denoting "WE" as a family and "WE" as without equal. This is a war-winning theme that would not let us go down in any battle…ever!

Please forgive me for taking such liberty with you, but you see, I believe that the human condition responds to such a challenge, and in this case, the "WE" theme sets the table for a will to win that is what? WITHOUT EQUAL. And most importantly, it speaks to family…the most important aspect of one's home life and workplace.

It invites reflection, thought, planning and action. I have learned that to move too quickly to action, even with a strong will to win, can invite failure. We need to be careful and not let the words "without equal" cause premature, ill-considered decision making. In my world, Gen. George Armstrong Custer had a very strong will to win in 1875 in that valley in Montana, and yet he and his cavalry troopers went down in one last stand!

Why? Precipitous bad judgment!

That was indeed Custer's last stand! I was determined in 1965 that Ia Drang was not going to be Moore's last stand. And you must be determined that the 21st century will not be your last stand!

The will to win is all about truth, development and one's personal journey. Developing the internal self is a rooted, structured process that begins with building from the ground "down" first, before building from the ground "up." The deeper one roots downward, the more strength one has to withstand life's hits and stay on a winner's course from the ground upward.

Are you aware of the tree structure of the most beautiful Live Oak? It spans the sky in its majestic and huge brilliance with shapely limbs. However, its root structure below the ground, what the eye does not see, reaches outward, not downward. When great winds come, it is not unusual for the mighty oak to have toppled on its side—only to reveal the surprise below. The root structure does not go deep enough to help it withstand major blows. It is truly a sad sight to see such beauty toppled so easily!

And, it can be with all of us. Our personal structure from the ground "down" should run deep, which then allows us to withstand the heavy winds that come our way. It is this structure that enables us to be "without equal." It leads to winning!

With "good leaders," he or she wins most of the time. With "great leaders," his or her men or women win all the time!

I wish to share an observation from my many years in leadership. Be cautious in determining who you believe the real "good" and "great" leaders are. There is no one profile that makes or breaks a leader. One may be quiet and reflective, or one may be passionate and full of vigor and fight. One may be six feet five, or one may be five feet six. One may have an advanced degree, or one may have a GED from high school. The will to win – to be without equal – is not particular in where it finds a permanent home!

But regardless the choice and pursuits in life, the requirements to have an authentic will to win are the same. Let us visit the matter of building and developing, even further, a will to win from the ground "down"... the invisible part of our nature and character. *Our personal experiences in life are quietly building, out of sight, our will.* How can one think about the components of the one's will – those aspects of life that can hopefully stand disappointments, failure and even brokenness – when one's will has not been broken?

Perhaps each of you has been a fortunate person who has always flown high without failure or disappointment. Well, I can tell you that my three stars earned in the military were due to my trust in my rooted mental infrastructure. There were days when my men were being killed to my left and right, I relied on my roots. When my wife died suddenly after 54 years together, I relied on my roots. When members of my family had a personal crisis, I relied on my roots. When my aging process reduces my physical ability to do things that I have always been able to do well, I rely on my roots.

It is now that I wish to discuss internal trusting of self, and how trust plays out in "without equal." There is a great term in golf, where golfers must repeat their swing over and over for a long time until they begin to trust their swing without even thinking about it.

As in golf, we must trust our swing, our rooted structure, without ever questioning it. When times are at their worst, one's trusted swing gets one back in the fairway of life and onto the green. Specifically, I shall mention three things that are built into my nature now, and hopefully, at 86 years, they are working as they should. These were my rooted structure priorities back then, and are still today.

- The development of one's mind.

- The condition of one's body.

- The nature of one's spirituality.

The mind must always be alert and in a learning mode. The body is your machine and ticket to winning. The soul matters more than one may believe or know. Each of these elements is part of my "trusted swing." It is all about balance in your golf swing and in the swings of life. Now, I shall speak to one's will to win, to be without equal, from the ground "up," from the visible aspects of one's nature and character. This is the hard part, the execution, where all of your training and trusted swings come into play. If your rooted structure is right, and you are in the right place at the right time, let it rip! Go for the green. Trust your swing and do not even think about it. This is where your balance comes into action...where the mind, body and soul function as one. What a beautiful sight to see.

Remember, it is never too late to work on your rooted structure. The invisible part of your life will always impact the visible. There is always one more thing you can do, that I can do to influence the situation in one's favor.

Let us revisit "WE"...without equal.

I cannot speak to this enough. Your bottom line is how you may be measured every day. You must have personal balance to have institutional balance. This is being deeply rooted from the ground down. This will impact your will to win from the ground up. This places you and your institution in a rare place – to be without equal.

WE! You are family. I am about family. All of us know what it takes to possess an authentic will to win...to be without equal...WE.

Thank you and "drive on!"

Made in the USA
Monee, IL
07 August 2021